D0374747

LAST POST

MAX ARTHUR is the author of the *Sunday Times* best-sellers and award-winning *Forgotten Voices of the Great War* and *Forgotten Voices of the Second World War*. His other oral history titles include the classic work on the Falklands Campaign, *Above All, Courage,* and the recently published *Lost Voices of the Royal Navy* and *Lost Voices of the RAF*. *Symbol of Courage; the History of the Victoria Cross,* was published in 2004. He is also the military obituary writer for the *Independent*.

LAST POST

MAX ARTHUR

PHOENIX

This book is dedicated
to those who did not return

A PHOENIX PAPERBACK

First published in Great Britain in 2005
by Weidenfeld & Nicolson

This paperback edition published in 2006 by Phoenix,
an imprint of Orion Books Ltd,
Orion Books Ltd,
Orion House, Upper St Martin's Lane,
London WC2H 9EA

13 15 17 19 20 18 16 14 12

Copyright © Max Arthur 2005
Picture section © Johnnie Shand-Kydd
All other photographs © interviewees and their families

All rights reserved. No part of this book may be reproduced or
transmitted in any form or by any means electronic or mechanical
including photocopying, recording or any information storage and
retrieval system without permission in writing from the publisher.

Max Arthur has asserted his right to be identified as the Author of this work.

The Orion Publishing Group's policy is to use papers that are natural,
renewable and recyclable products and made from wood grown in
sustainable forests. The logging and manufacturing processes are expected
to conform to the environmental regulations of the country of origin.

British Library Cataloguing-in-Publication Data.
A catalogue record for this book is available from the British Library.

'The Last Post' by Robert Graves is reproduced
with permission of Carcanet Press Limited

ISBN-13 978-0-3043-6732-0
ISBN-10 0-3043-6732-X

Printed and bound in Great Britain by
Cox & Wyman Ltd, Reading, Berkshire

The Orion Publishing Group's policy is to use papers that are natural,
renewable and recyclable products and made from wood grown in
sustainable forests. The logging and manufacturing processes are expected
to conform to the environmental regulations of the country of origin.

www.orionbooks.co.uk

Contents

Acknowledgements

I must first and foremost thank Ian Drury, the Publishing Director of Weidenfeld & Nicolson, for his inspired idea for the book and title. He has been hugely supportive throughout. His Managing Editor, Ilona Jasiewicz, could not have been more helpful, charming or conscientious.

Throughout my travels to meet the veterans, I was accompanied by the photographer, Johnnie Shand-Kydd. I felt the book needed an outstanding photographer to capture the spirit of the veterans. Johnnie brought his personal talent and professional skill to some extremely difficult situations. His photographs dignify the last days of these men and I thank him. I would also like to thank Ken and Letitia Adam for recommending him and for their support for the book.

No author could have been served by better researchers than Vicky Thomas and Joshua Levine. Vicky Thomas transcribed accurately and sensitively all my taped interviews, bringing all her editorial skill to bear on the first draft. She also maintained contact with the families and residential homes of the veterans and orchestrated the correspondence and personal photographs for the book. She always responded positively to the most troublesome of requests. She is now researching her own book, *The Naga Queen*. Joshua Levine has brought his considerable flair and editorial skill to this book, and I profoundly thank him. I am also delighted that his book, *Forgotten Voices of the Blitz and the Battle for Britain* will be published in 2006. I am indebted to them both.

I want to thank all the veterans who contributed their personal accounts to this book. I began the book on 4 August 2004, when there were twenty-one known British survivors of the Great War. The youngest, at 104, was Bill Stone, and the eldest, Henry Allingham at 109. Now only four of those interviewed survive.

I must also thank the families of all the veterans who gave unstinting assistance and never grew impatient with my requests for further details to enhance the accounts. I was also very impressed with the residential homes where the lives of these grand old men are enriched by the love and care they receive. I would particularly like to thank Charles Griffiths, who over many years had interviewed Alfred Finnigan a number of times, and who kindly allowed me to use his interviews. My thanks also go to Davina Vanstone, who made available to me her interviews with Smiler Marshall, which have enhanced his story. My brother Adrian was always on hand to help with information on various regiments, and I thank him. I would like to thank my dear friends Don and Liz McClenn, who saw me through my first book, *Above All, Courage*, 22 years ago, and still continue to give me their constant support, as does the broadcaster Susan Jeffreys.

In the writing of this book, my very dear friend Ruth Cowen has continued to give me a quality of friendship that has deeply enhanced my life. Her own book, *Relish, The Extraordinary Life of Alexis Soyer*, was published in June 2006.

As always, my friend Sir Martin Gilbert has been a constant source of encouragement and generosity, and I also want to thank Lady Gilbert.

My most profound thanks must go to Dennis Goodwin, the Chairman of the World War One Veterans Association, who has cared for and supported so many of the veterans in this book. His caring over the last twenty years for hundreds of veterans has no equal. Many of these remarkable men would have slipped away earlier had he not provided stimulation and fun in their lives, escorting them to such events as Palace Garden Parties and trips to the battlefields of France and Belgium.

Throughout the writing of the book my life has been enriched by the love and laughter of Lucia Corti.

THE LAST POST

The Bugler sent a call of high romance –
'Lights out! Lights out!' to the deserted square.
On the thin brazen notes he threw a prayer:
'God, if it's *this* for me next time in France,
O spare the phantom bugle as I lie
Dead in the gas and smoke and roar of guns,
Dead in a row with other broken ones,
Lying so stiff and still under the sky –
Jolly young Fusiliers, too good to die . . .'
The music ceased, and the red sunset flare
Was blood about his head as he stood there.

Robert Graves

Introduction

The inspiration for this book came from an idea of Ian Drury's, the Publishing Director of Weidenfeld & Nicolson. After he had read *Forgotten Voices of the Great War*, he suggested I write a book based on interviews with the last survivors of that conflict.

Only one person in the United Kingdom knew how many veterans survived and where they lived – Dennis Goodwin, the Chairman of the World War One Veterans Association. Dennis has kept a watchful and compassionate eye on the veterans for many years and he kindly gave me details of the twenty-one survivors. I then had the pleasure of visiting and interviewing these men. All had a story to tell. Some had told their story before while others were opening up after a lifetime of refusing to talk about the war. Throughout these interviews I emphasised that I wanted to hear about their life before and after the war. The personal accounts which follow are, wherever possible, in their own words. Some of the accounts are supplemented with additional material from their families or friends. All the accounts were sent to each veteran for checking – in some cases a close family member or carer read their story to them. Some made a few changes, mostly concerning names of friends or places, while others added extra material. Allowance, however, must be made for the age of these men and the frailty of their memories. Some could recall very little, and this is borne out in their stories. Had I visited them on another day, I may have found them more receptive – or less so – but that is the luck of the draw when interviewing centenarians. Memory of detail is seldom perfect, even in younger people. Where possible I have checked the details, but sometimes the facts are buried in time.

It has been both an honour and a pleasure to meet these remarkable men, and I have fond memories of those who are no longer with us. But what humour they all had! I particularly remember the wry smile of John Oborne, aged 104, when I asked him if he had had lice while in the trenches; 'No,' he replied 'they had me.' Now, ninety years on, these remarkable survivors remain united by a common belief in the utter futility of war. All are bound by the traditional values of comradeship and loyalty, but even today, still struggle to make sense of the lives they saw wasted.

These are their last words. I have been but a catalyst.

Max Arthur

LONDON, 10 AUGUST 2005

Alfred Anderson

5th Battalion (TA) Black Watch

Born 25 June 1896, *died* 21 November 2005

I was born on 25 June 1896. I had two older brothers, Dave and Jack, who were born in Chicago, because my father had been one of many Dundee men who got recruited to go and help with the building of Chicago and my mother followed him out there. They came back to Dundee before I was born, where my father continued as a joiner and undertaker and my mother went to work in the jute mill – like her four sisters.

I remember in those days we had gas lamps for light and coal fires at home – and we lived on a hill so the horse-drawn carts had to struggle up and down. I used to play outdoors, and one day I saw two soldiers coming down the road – it was 1902 and they were returning from the Boer War. They were so glad to be back; they picked me up and carried me on their shoulders down the road.

I went to Hill Street School in Dundee – but I didn't like it and was only there for a short time. It was in 1902 that my father bought his own joinery yard in Newtyle in Angus and we moved there –

that was the year my sister Maud was born too. When I was ten I got a job in my spare time, delivering milk from Denend Farm to people nearby. By the time I was twelve I'd saved up enough to buy a bike, and I used it to earn pocket money to do more milk deliveries – I used to have milk churns hanging off the handlebars.

I went to the Harris Academy in Dundee from the time I was twelve to when I was fourteen, and I used to travel into Dundee by train. I enjoyed reading, writing and especially drawing – at one time I thought I might become an architect. When school was over I used to go back to Kirkton Farm where my school friend lived, and that's where I got my interest in animals, especially horses. Most of all, though, I liked playing and watching football, and we used to go to see Dundee play on a Saturday.

When I finished school I started an apprenticeship with my brother, but he went to Canada – in fact both brothers did – before the war started. I decided to join the Territorial Army when I was sixteen – quite a few lads my age joined up. We didn't have family holidays and it was great fun to go to Montrose or Crieff for a week's camp every year. Our instructor, Max Beverley, had been in the Boer War, and he used to train the fourteen of us every Saturday afternoon in Newtyle. I remember our third camp at Monzie near Crieff in summer 1914 – we trained on Lee Enfield Rifles and did route marches. I was there with my friends Jock Mackenzie and Jim Ballantine – I don't think we thought much about a war to come, even though troops were mobilised all around us.

When war was declared, our battalion – the 5th Battalion, the Black Watch – was called up and after two months' training we left by train for Southampton in late October. I didn't give it too much thought; I was too young for that. We had a night there, then we

Sergeant Alfred Anderson, the last surviving Great War veteran of the Black Watch. With the 5th Battalion he was shipped to France late in 1914 and saw action at Loos and was wounded on the Somme.

sailed to Le Havre on a cattle boat – which was clean, but it really stank. We spent a night in a tented camp at Le Havre, which was bitterly cold. We couldn't wash in the morning because the water had frozen in the pipes. We were glad when they marched us up to the front – which took three days – but it warmed us up a bit. We got our billets in bits of farm steadings, if you could call them that, then we got to work digging trenches under the supervision of the Pioneer Corps. We soon heard the first bullets and men started being wounded and killed. Two of my mates from home were wounded. It was a shock, but I think because my father had been a joiner and undertaker that helped me in a strange way. I'd seen death before.

I remember the eerie silence that first Christmas Day. All the explosions stopped. We were billeted in a farmhouse at the time and we went outside and just stood there, listening – and remembering our friends who were gone and our people back home. We'd spent two months with the cracking of bullets and machine-gun fire, and sometimes distant German voices – but now it was quiet all around. In the dead silence we shouted out, 'Merry Christmas' – although none of us felt at all merry. We were so tired, we didn't have the energy to play football – and we were quite a way from the front lines, so we didn't do any of the mixing with the Germans that was so famous. The silence came to an end in the afternoon when the guns started again. The killing began again too. It was a very short-lived peace. Now, at Christmas, I think of that day in 1914 and remember all my friends who didn't make it. But it's too sad to think too much about it – it's far too sad.

On that first Christmas we got our Christmas box – a metal box filled with cigarettes. In it was a card which said, 'With best wishes for a Happy Christmas and a Victorious New Year, from the Princess Mary and friends at home'. I'd no use for the cigarettes, so I gave them to my friends. A lot of the lads thought the box was worth nothing, but I said someone's bound to have put a lot of thought into it, and I kept it. Some of the lads had got their Christmas presents from home, but I got mine late. I used the empty box to keep the New Testament my mother had given me. In it she had written, 'September 5, 1914. To Alfred Anderson. A present from Mother' – it fitted the box perfectly. That's the only thing I brought home from the war.

Conditions in the trenches were terrible. We slept on sandbags and there were rats everywhere. They used to gnaw through the phone cables so our communications were cut off. We often had to stand up to our knees in water and I got trench foot.

As well as normal duties, I was detailed to look after one of the officers – Lieutenant Bruce-Gardyne – and when he went away on a course I was posted for a while as batman to Captain Fergus Bowes-Lyon – the brother of the late Queen Mother. He was from Glamis, which isn't far from my home in Newtyle. I really regret that I never got to meet the Queen Mother and tell her about my time with her brother before he was killed at Loos in 1915. He was a fine young man. A meeting was mooted once when she was at Glamis, but she took ill and it never happened.

The Battle of Loos was dreadful for the Black Watch and casualties were very high – especially the first day, 26 September, when Captain Bowes-Lyon was killed among hundreds more of our regiment. You see, our bombardment wasn't strong enough to break the German wire or to destroy their machine guns.

I often had to go out with the officer to a listening post – out in

Alfred Anderson (seated, front row centre), born in 1896, was forty-three years old when the Second World War began, and was too old for active service. Instead he joined the Local Defence Volunteers and ended up organising and training the 'Dad's Army' in Newtyle.

no-man's-land. We'd crawl out to a position in a shell hole or a depression in the ground after dark, and stay there all night, listening for sounds of tunnelling or German activity in their trenches – then we'd crawl back to our lines at dawn. On one occasion we were entrenched in a listening post on the Somme front and I was brewing up some tea when a shell exploded over our heads, killing several of my pals and injuring many others – myself included. I was hit by shrapnel in the neck and shoulder, but I managed to crawl to the officers' dugout, where someone put a field dressing on it. I had to lie there all day bleeding and in a lot of pain until dark, when they could send out a stretcher party to get me back to the trenches. My wounds were properly dressed later at a field dressing station behind the lines, but then I had to wait for a wagon to take me back down the lines. My fighting days were over, but I'd been lucky just to survive. That day my dearest friends were left behind in that trench for ever.

After a very painful journey which took a night and a day, I arrived at the hospital in Boulogne. They stripped off my uniform and deloused me, gave me something to eat and a cup of tea, and the medical officer removed the shrapnel. At last the pain eased, and they sent me back to Britain for the first time since 1914. There were ambulances waiting for us at Dover, and I was put on a train for Norwich. As we went, there were women at each station where we stopped who handed out tea. The hospital at Norwich was full when I arrived, so I was taken to a village hospital nearby, and I spent two months there convalescing. At last I was well enough to go on leave, and I got the train to Newtyle. As I walked down Belmont Street, I saw my mother polishing the brass door fittings, and I crept up and waited for her to look up . . .

While I was home on leave I went to see the family who had the other joiners' firm in Newtyle. They had two sons about the same age as me and we'd always been good friends. Before the war we used to practise fretwork together – but they too had been called up. I'd heard that one of the lads had been killed, and I went to see his three sisters at their home. I said I wanted to express my condolences – but they were very frosty and didn't invite me in. I realised I wasn't welcome with them, and said, 'It's not my fault.' But they were quite clear. 'Aye, but you're here, and he's not.'

I soon got fit enough for duty and was sent to the infantry training camp at Ripon – and was promoted to lance corporal. After taking courses in musketry, physical training and a general course at Aldershot, I was appointed battalion instructor and seconded to the Queen's Own Yorkshire Dragoons. It was while I was at Ripon that I met my future wife, Susanna Iddison, who lived just outside the town. We married in St Andrew's Church in Kirkby Malzeard on 2 June 1917, and I had a week's leave to visit my family in Newtyle.

When the war finished they offered me the chance to sign on as a regular – with promotion to sergeant major. I was very tempted because I loved the comradeship of the army and enjoyed my work as an instructor – but there was the family joinery business to run. Both my brothers were in Canada and as my father had started to suffer from chronic asthma, he needed help. I gave up the army and we moved back to Newtyle, where we had six children – Betty, Jim, Minnie, Andrew, Christina and Neil – between 1919 and 1935.

I bought my first car – an Austin – in 1926, and we used it to go on holidays to visit my wife's family in Yorkshire and on trips around Dundee. We had one of the first phones in Newtyle – our number was Newtyle 57 – and my wife had the first electric cooker in the village. We did well – and my brother came back from Canada to join us. I decided to leave him in charge, and we moved south to Yorkshire so I could work as a journeyman joiner. Although the country was in depression, I was kept busy, often working in the evenings and on Sundays to make coffins, as my father had done. The miners in Yorkshire were so poor they were often starving – there were a lot of coffins needed at that time. All the same, it was a welcome change not to have the burden of the business and employees and I was sad when my brother went back to Canada in the early thirties and I had to return to Newtyle to take over the firm again.

When the Second World War started, my work was affected by timber rationing. All timber work had to be officially approved, and the new house project I was going to work on was cancelled. My younger employees were called up, but I was too old for active service, so I relied on small jobs instead. When I heard that they wanted ex-servicemen to form the LDV [Local Defence Volunteers], I volunteered and ended up as the principal organiser and trainer in Newtyle. We got called out several times during the war, when there was an invasion scare on the east coast, and we got the local Boy Scouts working alongside us – they joined in some of our exercises and acted as local messengers. They had the sorry job of delivering the news of local men killed, wounded or missing to their families.

After the war I took on my son to work with me and I also had an apprentice – but we were only a small, independent firm, and it was hard to keep contracts coming in. When I was sixty I went to work for Dundee City Council, and then later became clerk of works for Perth City Council and Crieff Town Council. Those were happy times – and we enjoyed the freedom of having time to ourselves after the children had left home. I didn't retire until I was seventy-nine in 1975, then two years later we reached our diamond wedding anniversary. By this time we had ten grandchildren and eighteen great-grandchildren who came to celebrate with us. When my wife died in 1979 – she was eighty-three – I moved to a house in Alyth opposite my daughter Christina and her husband, and I've lived there ever since.

I don't know what I have to thank for my long life – I've never been a drinker or a smoker, and I eat good food in moderation. But I've always liked to keep active. In November 1998, when I was one hundred and two, there was a reception and the French government presented the Légion d'honneur to four of us who had served in the Great War. That year the BBC invited me to take part in a programme called *Western Front*. But I didn't want to go over those old memories. It's over – it's passed. If I dwelled on what happened during those terrible times, I would never have lived to see the age I am now. I've tried to put all those thoughts behind me. I've no wish to revive them. But what I saw and went through still affects me, even to this day.

I did agree, though, to appear in a TV feature about those boys who were executed for desertion, or very minor offences. It was called *Shot at Dawn*. The families of these boys had been fighting to have them pardoned – but they should never even have been accused. They should be pardoned now, not only for their memory, but for the sake of their parents before, and their families, for they bear the brunt of it.

At the time of the war I didn't give the reasons much thought. I was too young for that, and it was all a kind of jaunt for us. It was a different kettle of fish once we got to the trenches. I saw fellows I knew dying around me, and all I thought about then was living. I've been trying to forget war for the past eighty or so years, but wars just keep happening, and it's ordinary folk who pay the price.

It doesn't do to look back. We lived for each day during the war – and even at my age, now, I do the same thing. I'm still looking forward. I'm more interested in what's happening now.

Looking back, I wonder, 'What did we gain?' We certainly lost a lot, and we're right back to square one now. I think men will always fight. War is needed, I suppose, to settle some things – but maybe there is a better way.

ALBERT 'SMILER' MARSHALL

1st Battalion, Essex Yeomanry · *Born* 15 March 1897, *died* 16 May 2005

My name is Albert – but Smiler is my nickname, and always has been since I joined up in 1915. I was born on 15 March 1897 at Elmstead, a small Essex village three or four miles from Colchester, about twelve miles from the sea – which I never saw until I was ten years old. My father, James William Marshall, was a farm labourer, and he married a local girl, Ellen Skeet. When I was young there were no cars, horses being the main means of transport. I remember the first car I ever saw, passing through Elmstead in 1908.

When I was very small, my father put me onto a wooden cart pulled by a billy goat. When I was two and a half, he put me on the goat's back. The goat didn't like that at first and he bucked me off. My father picked me up and showed me that if I sat facing the tail and kept my arms round him, I could stay on. After that, I progressed to a pony and later to a horse.

On most Sundays, my father took me to Colchester to see the soldiers parade for church. Each regiment had its own particular

24

marching music and I can still recall most of them. What excited me most of all was their red coats. Many of the soldiers had just returned from the Boer War and they were wearing all their medals. At one of the parades, my father was approached by a sergeant of the Devonshire and Somerset Yeomanry who wanted me to become their mascot, but he said no.

My mother, Ellen, was ill when I was young, so I started school when I was just two and a half years old, although I didn't go on the register until I was five. My brother drove me to school – he had an orange-box on wheels, and I used to sit in it, and he used to wheel me. I was four when my mother died – two days after Queen Victoria died. Throughout my school days I only missed three half-days, and received the bronze and silver medals for attendance before I left school at the age of thirteen.

The headmaster was a wonderful man who took a great interest in me and all the pupils. He taught everything, including football and cricket, gardening – and he was also the scoutmaster. The staff were a bit 'fishy' – a Miss Herring, a Miss Salmon and the head-master was Mr Whiting. They were all much loved by the pupils. Each teacher taught two classes. Twice a week the rector visited for the first hour. We started with a hymn and were told about all the historical events which had taken place on that day. Any trouble, and you got the stick. None of the boys mentioned this to their parents, as they might well have been belted had they done so. Most boys had an orange-box on wheels and when we were released from school, there was a rush down the hill to collect horse manure for the gardens.

I was a bit of a fighter at school. A boy who had been expelled from another school started causing problems in our class. The master took me aside and told me to deal with him, so I met him outside where he was bullying some of the smaller ones and I gave him a good beating. He was as right as rain after that and he wanted to be my friend but I wasn't having any of that. Perhaps we could do with a bit more of that today.

Manners were very important in those days. If the boys didn't raise their caps and the girls curtsey to the gentry, then we were given a lesson in manners.

In the winter, the older girls served cocoa at a cost of a penny for five days – a penny ha'penny if there were two in the family.

We used to have a day's holiday from school for picking pears, and for lifting potatoes, the whole family taking part. The only excursion was to an agricultural show at the White City – this involved a two-mile walk to the local station.

For play we had iron hoops, costing sixpence, and the girls had wooden ones. Both girls and boys played marbles. There were large glossy ones called alleys, while the girls played with smaller ones known as pimsells. The girls enjoyed hopscotch, while the boys preferred 'fox and hounds'. We'd choose three or four to be foxes and they would run off with a 2–4 minute head start and hide or keep moving around in a wood or field with long grass. The foxes had a piece of wool round their arm. After the foxes had gone the hounds had to find them and rip the wool off. This was supposed to be the end of their life. The foxes could blow a whistle or howl to give the hounds a hint. Then when all the foxes were caught the game ended. It could go on for hours. In spring, when the mothers were cutting wallpaper for re-papering, paperchases were popular.

The flower show was an important event organised by the school masters from Elmstead and the adjacent village, Great Bromley. The girls wrote out the Twenty-third Psalm, the best six being selected for the show. They did flower arrangements and showed pressed flowers and butterflies, while the boys showed the produce of their gardens – vegetables and flowers.

I clearly remember several of the villagers. There was Mrs Page, who sold sweets, biscuits and cigarettes. A strip of liquorice cost a farthing, a bottle of ginger beer a penny. There was a glass marble at the top of the bottle which was much prized as marbles were at a premium. The Watkinsons sold bacon, dripping and cheese – large round cheeses. Six carriers took the produce to Colchester – a distance of four miles. Mrs Pentney sold haberdashery, women's overalls, children's dresses, stockings – and also tins of bully beef and condensed milk and cake by the half-pound. It was here that the future Mrs Marshall was to work.

The bakery was run by two spinsters who baked every day, starting at 4 a.m. Three pony carts delivered bread to outlying farms. Milk from the farms was collected in milk cans – a penny for a pint of skimmed, or for a ha'penny, a pint of new milk. Water was obtained from the village pump, which really belonged to the village pub – The Bowling Green – where you could get beer direct from the barrel for tuppence a pint.

The blacksmith played an important part in the village, making metal hoops for the wagon-wheels, shoeing all the horses and repairing anything. Most of the villagers worked on the land – the village policeman went out rabbiting and pigeon-shooting, and the pigeons were shared out in the village.

My grandfather cut hair, and I used to hold the candles for singeing for him, for which I was rewarded with a penny ha'penny, whilst home-brewed beer flowed freely.

Guy Fawkes Day was one of the highlights of the year. Boys leading a donkey, all dressed as Guys, used to go round the village singing:

Remember, remember the fifth of November,
The gunpowder treason and plot.
I see no reason why gunpowder treason
Should ever be forgot.
With a dark lantern,
With a light match,
Holla, boys, holla, boys make the bell ring.
Holla, boys, holla, boys, God save the king.
If you haven't got no money, give us some beer
Guy Fawkes comes only once a year,
Bang, crash, wallop!

Then they let off fireworks with a cannon and real gunpowder.

On Boxing Day all the villagers assembled with their pets for an unusual race – pigs, goats, ferrets, donkeys, cats, dogs, tame mice and even a cockerel – all wearing a collar and on a lead. There can never have been a race like it! All through the village went this odd assortment of pets, finishing on the village green – the winner having to climb the greasy pole to try and reach the dead duck on the top.

Boys were always out to make the odd penny. In summer, coaches taking tourists to the sea passed through the village, and the boys used to call out, 'Throw out your mouldy coppers.' Boys fought each other for tuppence. One day I was set upon by four boys. On my return home, my father said, 'Now you have met your

Waterloo,' and he treated my swollen eyes with raw meat. Another method of making pennies was cutting watercress, which sold for a penny a bunch, and a penny farthing for as much as the customers wanted.

On leaving school there were few openings for girls, who nearly all went into service. The pay was 3/6 per week. Hours were long, and there was only one half-day off each week. For boys there were more openings. They could go into agriculture, or work for carpenters, carters, etc. If you were an apprentice, or you had a job to go to, you could leave school at thirteen – but if not, you had to stay at school until you were fourteen. After that, you had to leave whether you had a job or not. I was apprenticed to the nearest shipyard, so I left school at thirteen. I changed from knickerbockers into trousers. At the shipyard, I was working with a Yorkshireman who was making all these beautiful doors. All I was doing was handing him the screwdrivers and saws and different tools while he was doing the work. In other words, I was a first-class-carpenter's labourer. At the end of my first week's work, I had got 2/4 and felt quite rich.

One day, whilst trudging along home with an empty basket, Mr Dickens passed in his milk cart. I asked him whether he would give me a lift. He asked what I did, and suggested that I should come and work for him, plucking chickens and looking after his best pony. As I had ridden from such a young age, I was delighted, and for the rest of the summer I went with him on his milk round. When he was ill, which lasted for months, he asked me to drive the milk cart and do his round – a great experience at the age of thirteen. All those houses, and having to remember who had what and whether they had paid. Then on Sundays I took great pride in getting the best pony and trap ready to take Mrs Stead and her daughter to the Wesleyan chapel. My wages were 4/6 per week. I gave my sister 2/6 – the rest I kept, gradually collecting enough to have my first bicycle, with solid tyres, which I bought from my brother for 3/6.

Mr Dickens once promised to reward me if I could get half a pint of milk from one of his cows whilst he milked two, but I had no success. The cow was dry.

At fifteen, I managed to get a job at Wivenhoe Park, now the University of Essex. I had the pleasure of looking after two ponies, John and Coddy, and I used them for taking dairy produce to the big house. It was around that time, in 1912, that I heard that the *Titanic* had gone down, and with her my Sunday school master, who had taught me the words of my favourite hymn, 'Nearer My God to Thee'.

When the war started in France in August 1914, our daily lives in England weren't affected – not at all. But big airships called Zeppelins came over. I saw two or three come over, flying low, but they were fetched down.

My whole life changed when Lord Kitchener and the world heavyweight boxing champion, Jack Johnson, came to Colchester in 1915. They appealed for the young fellas to join up into a fighting unit called 'Kitchener's Army'. Kitchener was on all these placards – YOUR COUNTRY NEEDS YOU. My brother – my only brother – was the first one to join from the village.

The Devon and Somerset Yeomanry were stationed near us because our area would be the first line of defence if the Germans crossed the Channel and got to East Anglia. The Yeomanry had cavalry and they could move quickly. You've got to try and remember, at the beginning of the First World War, there was little mechanised transport – and not much in the army either. I wanted to join the Essex Yeomanry so in Christmas week I went to their office in Colchester to join up.

I knocked on the door and the sergeant major said, 'Come in.' He asked, 'Well, what is your name, and how old are you?' I told him I was seventeen. He said, 'I think you've made a mistake. What year were you born?' I told him 1897, so he said, 'Look, go outside that door and think it over.' When I got outside, a fellow came up and said, 'Hello! You going to join up?' I said, 'Yes. I want to go where there's horses.' He said, 'Well, I'm going to join the Royal Horse Artillery – why don't you come with me?' I said, 'I've been in there once, and the old sergeant major told me to go outside and think it over.' 'You don't want much thinking over. You can't get in until you're eighteen.' So, I knocked again. 'Come in,' said the sergeant major, 'what can I do for you?' I said, 'I'd like to join the Essex Yeomanry.' He said, 'Right, how old are you?' I said, 'Eighteen.' He said, 'What year were you born?' I said, 'Eighteen ninety-six.' He didn't query it at all. He just said, 'Fair enough.'

After that, the sergeant major said, 'You can go home for Christmas – come back here on 5 January 1915.' So of course this is what I did. I went and was attested into the Essex Yeomanry on 5 January 1915. Oh yes, I was very keen to join up.

I went to train at Stanway and I went into private billets. One day, at about six in the morning we were in a field doing physical jerks – arms up, trunk forward – bend – and there was snow on the ground. When the sergeant – Sergeant Beavis of Clacton-on-Sea – said 'Trunk forward, bend!', I bent down, and I was a bit of a lad – I threw a snowball at the row in front and it hit a chap up the behind. He jumped up, and so did two or three of the others. 'Ah! Very funny!' said the sergeant. 'You can break you mother's heart, but you won't break mine!' I tried to look innocent. 'Yes, son, I'm talking to you, smiler!' The next morning and whenever I met my pals, it was, ''Morning Smiler!' and that went right the way through the war. Letters and everything. Even to this day, wherever I go, I'm known as Smiler.

When I joined the Yeomanry, I was already a good horseman, so I soon passed my riding test. You see, when I was at school, there'd been a sergeant in the 16th Lancers in our village – he was a regular soldier – and we'd got a little paddock at the back of our house, and he'd got a nice roan horse there. He used to take me up in front of him on the horse. He trotted, then he cantered and then he let go. He was holding me with his two arms on the front of the saddle with him. After that, every time he came home, we used to ride – but what he didn't know was that when he wasn't at home, I used to slip out the back, jump on his horse bareback and have a little ride around on my own.

Within one month of joining the Essex Yeomanry – before I'd even turned eighteen – Captain Hayward spotted me and said, 'I can see you can ride. I'm bringing two of my hunters here next Saturday and I want you to look after them – and your own horse if you've got one, and the government will pay you for it.' So, I became groom to Captain Hayward and I got my own horse from the government. I also learned to ride side-saddle because Captain Hayward had a friend called Miss Bannister who lived a mile away. She rode side-saddle and I did not want to have to lead her horse.

The Essex Yeomanry had lost quite a few at Mons, and they wanted ten reinforcements, so at the end of the hunting season I volunteered for France and I was sent to the cavalry barracks at

Smiler Marshall and his wife Florence on their
wedding day in 1921.

Colchester to be trained with the 20th Hussars by Sergeant Rabjohn – said to be 'the smartest man in the British Army'.

At Colchester, you had to learn about the equipment and how to saddle up with different straps and you had to pass out in riding with the different bridles. We learnt to use a sword on foot and also on horseback for when the German cavalry was coming at you. You had to pass out with a rifle so we went on the rifle range. After that, we went to Southampton where we got some remounts. They had lost some horses in France, so we took a shipload of horses on the ferry across, and arrived at Le Havre. I joined my regiment in November 1915 at a small village in northern France. There I was billeted for some time, journeying to Abbeville for horses and rations. Our cooks there were a scream – Charlie Darling and Oscar Wilde! The joke at the time was 'Why was Oscar wild? Because they called Charlie darling.' It was all very silly.

The cavalry would be stationed about a mile behind the lines, all the way from Mons to Verdun – the whole length of the lines – and whenever the Germans broke through or tried to we were sent to stop them. Three out of four men in each section would dismount and these three would act as infantry and dig a hole from which to fight until the infantry came up. The fourth man would be left to take the other men's horses out of the way. You would lie in this little dugout and you could just see over the parapet – but you mustn't put your finger over the parapet or it would be shot off. You would hold your position until, at night, the pioneer battalion or Royal Engineers would come along and dig a trench just in front of you. They would work away with their duckboards so that within a day you'd have a new line of trenches. When the infantry arrived, you were all right. But in the meantime, it was up to us to stop the Germans.

At one battle, the Royal Horse Artillery came out of a little wood and galloped forward, jumped off their horses, turned the guns round and started firing away. You had the Royal Horse Artillery, Royal Field Artillery and the Royal Garrison Artillery firing at the German front line and reserve. The Field Artillery were in support while the Garrison Artillery fired at the arms and food dumps. Then the Germans started firing as well. We were in the middle. The German shells came over us and so did the British ones. Back and forth over our heads. We didn't get too many because we were very near to the front line, so they daren't do anything in case they dropped short. I remember all the different sorts of shells the Germans used – I've got a toasting fork hanging up in one of my rooms and on the handle are all the different nose caps off the German shells.

At this stage, whoever made a raid was stopped and neither side gave way. If the Germans made a raid, ten, twenty, fifty of them were stopped by machine guns – and if we made a raid, it was the same for us. So really and truly, nobody got very far. All that happened was that ten or twenty people were killed for no reason at all. Getting nowhere.

I experienced gas twice – and it's still with me now. The first time was mustard gas, and the second lot, I only got a whiff of it – goodness knows what it was. If you got a proper dose you wouldn't be alive, but as it reached us, blow my boots if the wind didn't change and it blew right back over no-man's-land – right back on the Germans. True as I'm here. That particular gas made my eyes water. You couldn't stop crying – water was running from your eyes. When we had the first lot of gas, we had a piece of muslin which we tied round the nose and mouth and round the backs of our heads. By the second lot we'd got gas masks which came right over your head. They were terribly hot and awful, but still, they stopped the gas. But the gas is still with me today. It makes me itch every morning and at six every night. You can see my skin is all dry. Tonight, my arm will itch from the top to the elbow. And so will the back of my neck. It feels like a needle pricking you. And that's from ninety years ago. I've got some ointment stuff that the doctor gave me, but that only eases it – it doesn't cure it.

We went from Mons to Ypres and from Ypres to Cambrai and Amiens. You can't mention anywhere – from Mons down to Verdun, Hill 60, the whole lot – that I haven't been. We knew it all. We were on the move the whole time. The cavalry moved from one place to another overnight, and the Germans couldn't find out who was against them. We moved to deceive them.

We got used to standing in a fire trench and trying to aim through a tiny hole, just big enough to get the rifle through. We used to watch there for the German snipers. When a German fired, you might see a little spark come out of the barrel, and you'd fire through that tiny hole and try to get him. I remember when Lenny Passiful, my best friend, said, 'Let me have a go, Smiler,' and he jumped onto the fire trench and put his rifle through that tiny hole. I saw him fall – I was in the trench close by him and I put my arm out and I caught him. His rifle stuck in the hole – but the sniper had got him, right through that tiny little hole. I laid him down and stayed with him until help arrived. When Geoffrey Weir, his sergeant, came along, I said, 'He's my best pal – let me take him to the communications trench.' The sergeant said, 'He's in my troop. I'll take him.' I begged him to let me take Lenny – I knew where the first aid place was – it was in a chalk pit that had been occupied by the French. But the sergeant took him and as he carried Lenny along, a trench mortar fell right on the parapet. It exploded and blew the parapets in, so the sergeant had to wait until that settled, and then he had to lift Lenny over it. For a fraction of a minute, he was exposed to the enemy. He got the DCM for that – for taking a wounded soldier to the first dressing station. Well, I said to Lenny, 'You're very lucky! You've got a Blighty One. I'll write to your mum in England.' It was awfully difficult to write – but I did. I wrote and said, 'Expect Len home any day. I broke his fall and he's got a Blighty One.' About four or five weeks later, I had a letter from Lenny's mum. She said that Lenny had died three days later. He never got back to Blighty. He's buried in Béthune Town Cemetery. His mother received some money from the army – but £1 was deducted for the blanket in which he was buried. Bastards. A pound for the blanket. How could they?

A few years ago I went to France, to Béthune, and I laid a wreath on his grave. So I know exactly where Lenny is. I think of him most days.

Sometimes, we used our swords, and funnily enough – even though the Germans were good fighters – as soon as they saw the swords, or the lancers coming at them with the horses, they skedaddled as fast as they could, back to their trenches. On one occasion there was a group of about a hundred Germans out on patrol. They were taken by surprise by our cavalry and scattered, but I watched as the cavalry charged them on horseback across an open field. They drew their swords and simply cut them down. It was cut and thrust at the gallop. They never stood a chance. The Germans wouldn't stay put against a cavalry charge. They scampered into the trench right quick, and into the tunnels.

I remember once watching the Bengal Lancers go into attack against them. The lancers didn't hang about. They never bothered with saddles – they just jumped on and galloped off. It was the only time I saw a lance used. They were born horsemen – magnificent. Thousands of miles away from home and yet in their element. Terrible thing, the lance.

The worst sight I saw in the war was Mametz Wood, where the Essex Yeomanry were held in the rear, ready to exploit the advance of the infantry. It was a small-scale Somme, if I can put it that way. There were two woods, and the German front line was on the edge of one wood, and ours was in the open, on a hill. It was about 200 yards long and 150 yards wide. The Ox and Bucks infantry had been sent out to Mametz village. They were beautiful, clean and smart because they'd just come out from England. I was in Mametz village with about twenty of our regiment on a working party. We were a bit muddy and rough. They'd taken us away from our troops and our horses. For two days and two nights, our artillery bombarded Mametz Wood and it was thunder and lightning – that's the only way I can describe it. There wasn't a tree or a stick left standing. The earth was blowing this way and that. Having spent the night in Mametz village, the Ox and Bucks went over at half past six in the morning. Their objective was to capture Mametz Wood. Well, they went over this short bit of no-man's-land in two waves. And by nine o'clock there were only a few of them left – nearly all of them were dead.

The next night, on our working party, we rolled their bodies into shallow holes and covered a little dirt over them. By the next day, there was nothing. You couldn't see them – just plain ground again. But all those men were under there, just a foot deep. All dead. I reckon Mametz Wood was the worst sight I saw in the war. I reckon so, and I saw lots of terrible things.

Of course it was upsetting but, like everything else, you see it as a matter of what comes to you. You wondered – and I think most of us did it – if you would be the next one tomorrow. That's all there was time to think about. The parson used to say a little prayer. He said it doesn't matter how near you are to death and what sort of muck and muddle you're in, he said, 'try and think there's somebody worse', and that still helps me today.

Nearly all of the communication trenches ran through a chalk pit that the Germans once held but our troops had taken back. Dugouts were made in the chalk – dugouts as big as the room I'm sitting in. When you were inside these dugouts, nothing could hurt you – shells, mortars – whatever, nothing could get you. Each cook had a dugout and in the corner they'd keep their stores – a sack of carrots, a sack of potatoes, a sack of onions, a sack of dates, a sack of currants, and a sack of rice. At 6.30 in the morning, two men were detailed off from each troop, and you went down a communication trench to the chalk pit. You gathered up two dixies and you filled one with plain tea and another with tea with milk and sugar. And you brought them back to the thirty-two men in your troop.

The stores were brought up by the Army Service Corps. They brought up food for the troops and the horses. Boats used to sail from England to Le Havre and Dieppe full of provisions. The Army Service Corps' horse-drawn carts met these boats and took the contents to the dump at Abbeville, where they would be left at the stores. From there, a horse and truck would pick up the daily rations for the horses and troops and deliver them to the cooks in the chalk pit, where a little fire was going. After two years, the corps became mechanised and stopped using horses.

We were on the Somme from the first day of the battle – 1 July. We were in Mametz village, in broken-down houses with all the roofs and windows out – eight or nine of us in a room. Again, we were there in reserve to support the advance as best we could. On one occasion, we lay down there in the pouring rain and we stayed dry. We thought the Germans wouldn't venture out to make a raid in the pouring rain – nobody would be fool enough to do that. Raids were made just after a bombardment, so you knew that whilst a bombardment was going on, the Germans wouldn't attack. But the minute the bombardment stopped, up you all jumped to your guns, right quick, because you were expecting them to come over. You got used to what was going on. When you heard 'every man for himself', you cleared off to the communication trench and into your reserve or support. That way, when the Germans took the front line, they didn't capture anybody because before they got there, everyone had scarpered. You slid off down the communication trench to your next line of support. If you had to leave your machine guns, you took what we called the lock – that's the most important thing in the machine gun, and you can't fire it if you take the lock out. You take the lock out quick, and run down the trench into the commu-nication trench and you're out of the way. The Germans could capture the front line and the guns – but they ain't got the lock – so they can't fire them. Their locks were no good for our guns – and ours were no good for theirs. But the Jocks – the Cameron High-landers – the Scots, they were devils. As soon as they came in, if the Germans had taken our front line, they couldn't wait to get at them.

During a battle, you couldn't tell how many were killed on either side. All you knew was what your part was. There could be a terrible battle going on no further away than the end of your lane, but you wouldn't know until you were told next morning that your mate was killed. You'd only know the part of the battle that you could see but the rest was just a matter of shells bursting here, bursting there, bursting everywhere – and you couldn't get out of the way of them. It wouldn't have mattered what you did. So really and truly you never thought beyond the area that you were in. Now and then it would become quiet, but you could hear them catching it a little further away. You knew people were getting killed but you couldn't tell how many. You lost people every day.

When I was due for leave, the Germans pushed – so they said all leave was stopped. That happened to me three times. Eventually I think I'd been there about eighteen months when I finally got home to England for a week – that was the only time. Just once during the war. On my return to France, we had an idyllic interlude. The brigade was recuperating at Paris Plage, swimming in the sea – both ourselves and the horses – and boxing at night. I won a few matches.

We used to enjoy a singsong – and if the wind was in the right direction, you could hear the Germans singing back. In the front line we used to throw the Maconochie's bully beef tins over into no-man's-land. It used to encourage the rats. Maconochie bully beef was named after James William Maconochie and he shared my father's initials – James William Marshall. So I made a little song up:

James William Maconochie ran a cannery on his own,
Beans mixed up with turnips and carrots and all sorts of things.
The troops thought it a funny one,
When an onion came to life,
But the troops didn't mind that
But the man who got fat,
It was JWM.

To the tune of 'D'you ken John Peel' I made up this one:

> *D'ye kill old Smiler with his coat so grey,*
> *D'ye kill old Smiler at the break of day,*
> *D'ye kill old Smiler when he's far, far away,*
> *With his hounds and his horn in the morning?*
> *For the sound of this horn brought me from my bed*
> *And the cry of his hounds that he oft-times led,*
> *For old Smiler's 'View hallooo' would awaken the dead*
> *Or the fox from his lair in the morning.*

Then there were others that we all sang:

> *If the sergeant pinched your rum swearing blind,*
> *If the sergeant pinched your rum never mind,*
> *He's entitled to a tot,*
> *But he drinks the bloomin' lot –*
> *If the sergeant pinched your rum never mind.*

And:

> *I want to go home, I want to go home,*
> *The cannons they roar and they roar and they roar,*
> *I just don't want to go up the line any more.*
> *Will you take me over the sea,*
> *Where those Germans cannot get me,*
> *Oh, I don't want to die, I want to go home.*

We used to sing this one with great gusto hoping it would happen:

Take me back to dear old Blighty,
Put me on the train for London town,
Take me over there,
Just drop me anywhere,
Birmingham, Leeds or Manchester,
I just don't care,
For I shall be off to see my best girl,
Cuddling up together we soon will be,
Well, hi-tiddly eye ty,
Take me back to Blighty,
Blighty is the place for me.

We were always thinking of home:

H stands for Happiness that you should find there,
O stands for old folks in the old armchair,
M stands for Mother, you'll never find another, no matter where you roam,
E stands for everyone and as everyone knows,
H.O.M.E. spells home.

And of course the old favourites: 'It's a long way to Tipperary'. We sang them all, 'Mademoiselle from Armentières' and all that sort of thing. It kept up our spirits and kept away the boredom.

I was wounded at Mametz Wood and I landed up in Rouen Hospital, with a bullet through my hand amongst other wounds. The boat bringing the wounded back docked at Newcastle, and I was sent to convalesce in Eastbourne. They dressed me in blue with a white shirt and red tie so that everyone could see that I'd been wounded. When I had recovered, they sent me to Aldershot to retrain because they didn't think that I could handle a horse any more. I felt as though they were playing at strangers so I volunteered for the Machine Gun Corps at the first opportunity. I got to France, despite problems in passing the medical. At Le Havre I had to become a machine-gunner. After moaning and groaning I did the course and I was posted to the Leicestershire Yeomanry to support a brigade of cavalry, which entailed much outpost duty. My twenty-first birthday was spent in a derelict farm shelled by the Germans, and our gun crew had to melt snow for our tea.

I fought with the Machine Gun Corps at Hill 60. The Germans made a raid first on one side and then on the other, and they tried to come through to capture the lot of us. There were eight machine guns up there, and I was on one of them. They came in from both angles, but our outside guns spotted them and we just mowed them down. They kept coming up that hill, though. They were very brave. Our machine guns used to fire 240 rounds a minute – and you could alter the fuse spring and make it fire quicker if you wanted to. The gun was carried along by a two-man crew and boxes of ammunition were carried by pack ponies. It wasn't that I specially liked being on the guns but you took things in your stride. Everybody was a bit scared, but that's how it was. If a shell burst a few yards away, that made you jump for a minute, but you got used to it.

We were at Thiepval in 1918. We took a big piece of no-man's-land – terrific size – and we covered it with machine guns, right the way up to the three woods that covered the Somme. Then we saw a squadron of the Third Dragoons, I think it was, come through one of the woods and they made a charge across. We don't know what happened, because the Germans scarpered. They were quick to get back into their trench. They always had tunnels running right underground from their front line to their second line so they could get away. We didn't have those tunnels, we just had dugouts because we never stayed in them long enough. But the Germans were always in theirs – they'd always got a whole regiment of German soldiers smoking, laughing and singing, ready at any time – ready to make a raid.

That was where we were on 21 March 1918 when the Germans advanced. Had that first day of their advance been a success, the war would have been over before – but it wasn't. Then we were up and down, along the side of the woods – in the woods, out of the woods – on the move all the time, so if the Germans shelled, we weren't there, because we'd moved. Then their intelligence noticed where we'd moved to. As soon as the shells came over, we moved again. The whole thing was complicated, and only if you were there could you see what was happening. We just got out of sight as quick as we could. Beyond the wood you had a deep trench with a big, tall parapet that side, and a big, tall parapet this side – and you're five or six feet down and you're all right. Of course, if a shell burst there – well, you'd be done for. The pieces that fly off are red hot when they explode, and they'll cut your arm or your head off – take your face off, your nose or your ear – anything.

We used to try and write letters home but – oh crikey. Say that you've got an envelope and a writing pad – well, it poured with rain and it got soaking wet and that was no good. Even if you managed to write – well, you couldn't stick it all down because it had to be censored by the officer. The best thing was the Salvation Army. They used to come right up to the support about half a mile from the front line under shell fire with a pony covered-wagon – and they'd bring oranges and bananas and cigarettes – and if you were lucky you could buy a tin of fifty Gold Flake or fifty Players. Besides that, we used to get two packets of ten and a box of matches once a fortnight. They were horrible things – I couldn't smoke 'em. But you could sell anything, and chaps'd give you two francs for one cigarette. I bought my fifty and I was well away. I tell you what I did – my water bottle never had a drop of water in it all through the war. I used to swap my fags for the rum rations. The sergeant would come along with a spoon of rum and in the front line you had to drink it – but beyond the front line you could do what you liked with it. Once the officer and orderly sergeant had gone past, I used to take my socks and boots off and rub the rum into my feet. You weren't supposed to take your boots off. First, I'd lick a bit – it was very strong and it took your breath away. Then I'd rub me toes and feet. That's the reason I've got good little feet now – smashing. I've got a smashing little pair of feet.

I remember once seeing that a mule had been killed by an explosion. Our cook tried to break the routine of hard tack biscuits and bully beef by seizing the remains of the mule and frying it up. God only knows what we were eating but it tasted good. Another time, we watched the Australians arriving fresh for the fight. They cleared their mess wagon and as soon as they were out of sight, we climbed inside and scooped up the crumbs of bread and slivers of cheese that they'd left behind. I used to hate cheese but I've liked it ever since that day.

One day I was in a trench just eighteen yards from the nearest German trench, when the Germans sent a stick grenade flying over. They'd tied a couple of cigarettes to the grenade. After a bit, I went over to it. My mates said, 'For God's sake, don't touch it.' They thought it would go off and blow me up. But I went ahead and smoked one of the cigarettes and it was all right – so we sent the same stick bomb back with a whole packet attached. I hope they enjoyed them.

Another time, a shell landed close by me and I was buried up to my waist in thick mud, unable to move, and I was sinking. It was hopeless but I kept singing, and I managed to attract a search party by singing 'Nearer My God to Thee'. They pulled me out, but my two comrades were never seen again. That shell hole became their grave.

I think the worst thing of the whole war was being so lousy – we hated the lice. You could take your shirt off and you had a candle – they'd give you a candle and a box of matches every week or every fortnight – and you got in this little dugout – just a hole in a trench – and you lit the candle. You took your shirt off and you'd run the seams along the flame of the candle, and it would kill off all the eggs. You could do that today, but you'd be just as bad tomorrow. Terrible, terrible. If you asked me the worst thing about the war, I would say it was the lice. The shells didn't worry me – the snipers didn't worry me – the Germans didn't worry me. The lice worried me. You were smothered with them. And it was everybody – the officers were the same – it didn't make any difference. In fact they got them all the more, because they had cleaner clothes than we did. I was filthy – I only had two baths in three years. As for the rats, they were big blooming things. They used to sit there and look at you and more or less ask for food. We had all the ammunition we liked so sometimes to amuse ourselves we used to have a shot at the rats as they ran along the parapet.

The officers were smashing – they were just like ordinary troops.

It wouldn't do for an officer to have any bull, oh no, because next time he went up to the line he'd get shot – by his own men. And that certainly did happen. You'd have to be careful – you mustn't fall out with anybody, and that went for the officers and the sergeants as well. I knew of cases where it happened. You'd say, 'Oh, old what's-his-name got shot last night.' 'Yeah?' 'Well, they don't know how.' Or 'Sergeant so-and-so, somebody shot him last night.' You'd hear of it, yes.

There were punishments at the front. There was Number One Field Punishment. I remember this fellow – Barber. He threatened the sergeant or some such thing, so his hands and feet were tied with a strap to a wagon wheel. I was on guard through the night. I was guarding him and the rows of horses. Well, he wasn't able to move so I went along and put a fag in his mouth and lit it. After the war, I was in London one day and I ran into him. 'Good God! Is that Smiler?' 'Yes,' I said. 'Barber?' 'Yes.' He was now an insurance agent and he took me to a posh hotel and we had a wonderful tea. He said, 'I'll never forget you as long as I live. You saved my life.' Of course, they'd have tied me up too if they'd found out I was helping him – but they didn't. He said, 'You're a marvel.'

I never saw anyone being shot for cowardice. But when it happened, only one man in the shooting squad would get a live cartridge so the people firing didn't know who'd killed him. You'd never know which one out of ten had killed the man.

With regard to conscientious objectors – well you can't blame them as far as that goes, because they didn't believe in killing. There was a proper camp for them, and they had to do all sorts of fatigues – carve the rations – do all the dirty work. They worked in canteens and hospitals, they cleaned the barrack rooms, scrubbed and did all sorts of things. If you were a conscientious objector, you didn't go near the line – but you had to work.

At the end of the war, the Germans were on the run. Of course, our cavalry could move quickly, and every time the Germans saw our horses coming, they'd move on, and we were advancing two or three miles a day. On 10 November 1918, we advanced to Lille in France – and that's as far as we got. The officer came along and he shouted to the troops. He said, 'The war is over. There'll be an armistice tomorrow!' You never heard so much grumbling and swearing in all your life, because we'd got them on the run. We wanted to drive them back to Berlin.

On the day of the armistice, my unit was inside a factory in Lille. In the afternoon, we moved off and as we did so the factory was blown to smithereens. It had been booby-trapped. That would have been bloody ironic, being blown up on Armistice Day.

After the armistice, we could go to the stores and collect a new pair of breeches, a new pair of boots – anything we liked to make us look smart. We spent three days at Lille and then we went on into Germany. I was on the first machine gun guarding the Rhine at Cologne. That's as far as we went. We were on one side of the river and the Germans were on the other. That's where we stopped, then went back into Belgium and had a jollification – a singsong and a dance or two. After that, I became a groom to Kenneth Stroud. Being a regular soldier, he tried to get me to sign on and go out to India, where he was to be posted. Instead, a friend and I signed for one year in the Army of Occupation in Germany – and I got £50 for signing on. I stayed there for about eight months, with the Eighth Machine Gun Squadron.

In Germany we met some Fraüleins. You weren't supposed to

fraternise, but we used to stop and have a yarn with them. I can *parlez* a bit of the language – not much, but sufficient. I can speak enough French and Flemish and German to get around. I found most of the Germans very friendly. They took it. Shall I put it that way? We'd have been the same. They knew they were beaten and that was the end of that, so they were as nice as they could possibly be. They were all right.

The Germans cried when we left and they filled our water bottles with schnapps. They wanted souvenirs from us – buttons, badges, etc. To use up our German money we bought razors and scissors and that kind of thing. Then we came through Belgium and France, to Southampton – and very sadly we parted from the horses, handing them over to the Veterinary Corps. The Eighth Machine Gun Squadron was sent to Ireland where there was a lot of trouble. In Dublin shots came from all quarters, and I thought my end had come. Every morning I used to read the army notice boards, and one morning I saw that an officer's groom was required in the Curragh. I took this post and became groom to Major Moncrieff of the Machine Gun Corps for the rest of my time in Ireland until I was demobbed.

Major Moncrieff gave me a letter to give to whom it may concern, as a reference for a job. I received my gratuity of £26 10s for five years' service, plus £50 for the one year's occupation. Now I was homeward bound to civilian life and to my sweetheart Florence, who I married. I had lost most of my pals. The year was 1921.

I first met Mr Crossman soon after my demob. He was a captain in the yeomanry, who lived at the Hall at Great Bromley. He suggested that I should see the stud groom, who lent me his best horse. When I returned this horse, he asked if I was married. When I said

'Yes' he asked to meet my bride. He then showed me the founda-
tions of a bungalow, and asked if we would be interested in looking
after his horses, and living in the bungalow. This, our first home,
was a lovely bungalow in a large orchard at Great Bromley, about
two miles from Elmstead – my birthplace. A small hamlet, a church,
an alehouse, and one general store. In those days everything was
brought to the door – the butcher and the baker both called with a
horse and cart. For our first Christmas together, my wife and I were
given half a pig, which my young wife pickled, and six Plymouth
Rock speckled blue and white chickens.

Mr Crossman was the master of the local foxhounds, so when
the hunting season started, I rode to hounds. I had a full-time job
either hunting or looking after the horses. The kennel man taught
me a great deal. He was an expert with animals, and the farmers
brought him all their sick animals. From him I learnt much about
caring for them – especially horses. When the hunting season was
over, I helped the stud groom – a Mr Bantick – with brood mares
and foals, and a bay shire. I schooled three- and four-year-olds, and
eventually I rode all the horses in the show ring. On Sunday when
there was no riding, the stables were a real picture – blue and red day
rugs with the Crossman initials, pillar reins in white, bright brass
fittings – all the horses' manes plaited. I helped three different
masters of foxhounds – Mr Crossman, Colonel Guy Bluett and
Sir Harold Nutting. Hunting days were long, and we often had a
long way to hack to the meet, and then home again at the end of
the hunt.

On 8 December 1922 my first child, a daughter, was born. There
were to be four more, including twins. As we did not believe in vaccination, none of the children were vaccinated. In 1926 came the

General Strike. In those days the village bobby went about on foot – or on a bike – and knew practically everybody by name. As he was called away to the north of England to deal with the strike, I became a full-time police constable for the duration – which was quite an experience! I used to bicycle to the police station at Manningtree. One day there was a message from Sir Frederick of the Lodge, complaining about sheep-worrying, which I was asked to investigate. George and Ben, two bachelors who lodged at the Spread Eagle, said that they had seen a greyhound troubling sheep. I met the greyhound's owner, and sadly the dog had to be put down. After that, some of Sir Frederick's lambs were stolen, and I was again asked to investigate. Having got as much information as I could from the shepherd, I went to the pub, where I was told that Ben knew who had the lambs. I gave Ben and George a pint each, but no further information was forthcoming. The sergeant suggested I should go to the pub in civvies. More ale – but no more information as to the culprit. Finally the sergeant went to the pub, knocked on the door and asked for Ben. All Ben would say was, 'Sir Frederick *had* them, but he hasn't got them now.'

When the General Strike was over, I returned to my ordinary duties. Sadly, Mr Crossman died. All the staff acted as pall-bearers at his funeral. I stayed on with Mrs Crossman and the children until all the farms were sold. On my behalf, Mrs Crossman advertised for a new job for me. There were forty-three answers, but twelve said 'no encumbrances'. I eventually went to work for Captain Mumford at East Thorpe – a farm with surrounding land and a cottage which was too small for us. So, Captain Mumford suggested it could be pulled down and a new house built. The village had about one hundred inhabitants, no pub or shop and a bus into Colchester once a week. Soon after my arrival, Captain Mumford went to America, leaving me in charge of the stables. I was to use my own discretion as to whether I hunted or point-to-pointed the horses.

Whilst he was away, the officer in charge of the Royal Mews came to see me. He inspected the stables, and without hesitation suggested that I should go to work with the Windsor Greys, giving me six months to decide whether to accept the post, as the Windsor Greys were to be reformed on the accession of George VI. A cottage went with the job, and it would give the opportunity of entering royal service. Unable to get in touch with Captain Mumford, I could not accept the job.

On his return, Captain Mumford told me that he had bought a place in Surrey – a farm in Farley Green and a little cottage. He was moving there, and asked if my wife and I could move there with him. The chauffeur told me if I went to Surrey, I would never want to leave the county. Captain Mumford remarried – a farmer's daughter, who did not believe in blood sports – so he became a member of the drag hunt [where a scent is laid by a human, and there is no live quarry], along with his wife.

In 1939, I was clipping a mare ready for the winter hunting season, and while hogging her a hair pierced the lens of my eye. That day the drag hunt met at Farley Green, and I had made the course, so out I went. Unfortunately, a branch hit the same eye, causing a septic ulcer. Within two or three days I went to see an eye specialist in Shere and he sent me to Guildford Hospital. There I was treated with M and B 693 tablets. Unfortunately these didn't work, and an operation to remove the eye was needed. Before I recovered, the Second World War had broken out, so everyone who could be sent home was. My elder son Cyril took on my job, but as Captain

Mumford owned a hotel in Kenya, he decided to go there, and all the horses were sold for £60 each. Having written a testimonial for me, he said I might stay on in the cottage until I had another job. I went into the local Home Guard, and I patrolled Albury and Blackheath. A German plane came down, but by the time the Home Guard arrived on the scene, the plane was in flames.

During Captain Mumford's absence, his mother had power of attorney. Her visit to the local solicitor resulted in my receiving a letter stating that I should vacate the cottage within one month. I managed to get a job with the Donkins at Winterfold, then, after three court appearances, the eviction order was extended – by seven days. The captain in the Home Guard asked the solicitor to rescind the order. When my wife told Mrs Mumford that two of the children were ill, she retorted, 'Will your husband take the first job that is offered with accommodation?'

In 1940 I had been off work with fibrositis for five weeks and had nothing: Workman's Compensation was 18/- a week, of which 9/- was taken off for the cottage rent. The local council gave me a loan of £2 per week for my wife and three children. When I passed through Ashstead, I noticed a sign for the riding school, and I saw that there was a job going. I dressed smartly for the interview: navy suit, highly polished shoes and gleaming car. When I drove into the farmyard, I saw a man whom I took to be a gardener or yardman. As I got out of the car, the man raised his cap and said, 'Can I help you, sir?' I replied that I had come to see Mr and Mrs Maples, the owners. To my surprise, the man said, 'Are you Marshall, and is that your good lady in the car?' It was only then that I realised *he* was Mr Maples, the owner. I thought I'd lost the job before I'd even started. 'Come along,' he said, and off we went. We were given a nice lunch and shown all over the place and the cottage in Agates Lane. When asked by my wife if I thought I could do the job, I replied, 'I could do it standing on my head.' I was given a list of duties, such as looking after the car; cleaning gutters and drains regularly; being in charge of about thirteen and a half acres; keeping all waterways clear; rectifying any damage caused by ponies; collecting rent from the house opposite and from the three garages, and arranging for ex-servicemen to have land opposite as an allotment; ordering fuel for the house and garden boiler and looking after the ponies for the girls.

I was in the Home Guard with Mr Maples and we had many chats together – he had lost his two sons in the first war. Mr Maples suggested that, were we both alive at the end of the war, I should have his old home and stables rent free for three years. Sadly, Mr Maples died in the autumn of 1941, so I carried on at Murrey's Court Farm.

In addition to the duties, there were twenty hens, and a goat called Mabel, who produced triplets – Hop, Skip and Jump. As the war went on, things changed. The handyman, Frank, joined the RAF, so I took on his duties, including cleaning all the family boots and shoes, and looking after the girls' bicycles, etc.

During the first four years of the war, there was a great deal of bombing, and I saw many dogfights overhead. In 1942, I bought an eleven-year-old pony – Tommy – and a coster's cart, as petrol was rationed. I also bought a small plough and harrow with which to plough one acre of land, where I grew potatoes for which I received £10 from the government. I reared chickens, cockerels and geese, which I prepared for the table each Christmas. The surplus lettuces which I grew, I put out in a large bath, saying 'Help Yourself, 8d each'. The money was thrown into the bath which was in the road, and not a single penny was stolen.

One night, a German bomber jettisoned a whole canister of incendiary bombs on the garden. Fortunately, not one landed on the roof of the house, but the whole garden was ablaze. The first person out to help to beat out the fires was Mrs Maples. One bomb caused an elm tree to be taken up by the roots, leaving an enormous crater. Here we later planted two chestnut trees.

As things improved and the war moved towards its finish, I bought Star – a Welsh cob – and she was unmanageable. But she became an excellent jumper, won a number of trotting races and lived to thirty-seven. In fact, when I was eighty-five, I won a veteran class at a local show riding her.

Murrey's Court during the war had been more or less self-supporting, but afterwards things began to return to normal. The garden was used for events and the Scout and Guide fete was held there for some twenty-eight years. There were also Conservative fetes, the annual flower show with a marquee in the field, and even a small circus. In 1961 there was a terrible thunderstorm on the day of the flower show with very tragic consequences, as a girl and two horses were killed by lightning.

Every night at Murrey's Court, I used to make a tour around the stables, garden and horses to make sure that everything was in order. One night, dressed in my white shirt, I went round a little earlier than usual and Alice, the housekeeper, spotted me. But she didn't recognise me, and told Mrs Maples, who dialled 999. As I passed the chicken hut, I spotted someone flashing a light all over the place so I picked up a large stick and quietly followed the light. I waited until I had the man cornered and I shouted and raised my stick to hit him, only to find it was a policeman who said he was looking for a man in a white shirt seen prowling around the grounds.

As soon as petrol became available, my old Wolseley was on the road again, and I used to take soldiers to Sandhurst. Once the children had married and moved away, my wife and I had our first holiday – on our 25th wedding anniversary. We went to a guest house in Bognor.

One of the highlights of my life was when the caretaker of the Peace Memorial Hall came to visit, bringing a ticket for the Armistice celebration at the Albert Hall, in which the Ashstead British Legion were represented. At the coronation celebrations in 1953, I dressed in my scarlet and led the procession to Ashstead Recreation Ground. I blew the hunting horn from the time I left Murrey's Court until we reached The Leg of Mutton. There, the door opened and I rode into the pub and blew my horn again. I also kept a promise I made to a friend of mine – an Essex farmer – that if I was in England when he died, I would attend his funeral in hunting pink – and this I did.

Many of the girls I have helped with their riding and general stable management are now married, but they keep in touch and visit me when they are passing through – some from as far away as America and New Zealand.

I have seldom had a vet, as in the past I made all my own medicines, physic balls, etc. I had sixteen well-tried recipes, and could get anything from the chemist – which is unfortunately impossible today. The most important point when treating a sick horse or a wounded one is to be confident in the treatment you are giving. Generally in the past, whatever arose, I could usually cope with.

There have been many changes in those helping to keep the garden and grounds, including at one time the hiring of two Italians, one of whom is here today. My son used to cut the grass. We have never bought manure, and I have generally mixed my own potting soil.

I have kept good friends with the gypsies, giving them things such as bales of straw. We never turned anyone away and approved all religious denominations. My wife had been a keen Sunday School teacher, and I never remember her swearing – and I don't know what she would have done had I sworn in her presence.

As time went on, we said goodbye to two old friends who worked in the house – Tanner, the very correct parlour maid, who was a great stickler for etiquette, and Alice, who had joined the household as a housemaid many years before and had helped out with the cooking when Mrs Maples sacked the cook, who had a terrible temper. She continued as cook for countless years, until ill health caused her to retire. Things never seemed the same in the house after these two loyal members departed. I even thought of buying a home, but neither my wife nor Mrs Maples would hear of this, so I am still in the same cottage in Agates Lane.

For most of my life I did not speak very much about the war, but in my nineties I joined the World War I Veterans Association, of which I am now vice-president. Upon turning one hundred, life really took off for me. Shortly after my hundredth birthday in 1997, I went with a party of sixteen veterans to Passchendaele for the 80th anniversary of the battle in 1917. This was attended by the Duke of Kent, the President of the War Graves Commission, who lost a father himself in the Second World War.

In 1998, at the age of one hundred and one, I went to 10 Downing Street with a dozen other veterans, and we met Cherie Blair. Then in November of that year, I travelled to Béthune with

Sir Harry Secombe to lay a wreath on the grave of a pal who was killed fighting with me – Len Passiful. This was filmed for *Songs of Praise* and broadcast on Remembrance Sunday. That same month, November, I was presented with the Légion d'honneur award by a French general at the Imperial War Museum. I was then interviewed live on Richard and Judy's television programme – keeping my hat on!

In 1999 I made the final pilgrimage of the century with nine other veterans to Ypres and to Paris, where we laid a wreath at the Tomb of the Unknown Warrior. Channel 4 were filming a series about changes in country life during the twentieth century, called *Green and Pleasant Land*. Having lived through the entire century and being a dyed-in-the-wool country bloke, they chose me to take part and this was broadcast just as the millennium changed.

In 2000 I sang trench songs at a classical concert in Rochester Cathedral, getting a three-minute ovation at the end! At the age of one hundred and five, I was special guest of the Queen Elizabeth's Foundation at a classic car show in Leatherhead, where I was interviewed for the ITV news programme, *London Tonight*.

In the spring of 2003, my son John and I and eight other veterans met Prince Charles at the National Archives in Kew, where we were handing over for posterity documents relating to the war. He showed great interest in all of the veterans and asked me particularly about my lifelong love of horses. Then later that year I was filmed with children from Haslemere School for *Newsround*, the children's news programme on the BBC. This went out on Armistice Day, helping today's young people not to forget the sacrifice of my comrades.

Only last year, I appeared along with Cecil Withers in a Channel 4 documentary *Britain's Boy Soldiers*, being one of those who lied about their age to join up. It subsequently won the Best Factual Documentary category at the Royal Television Society's awards.

Today, very few people want a garden and hard work is out of the question. There's not the same comradeship today as there was, although I have always been very fortunate, surrounded by my good lady, my horse people, my five children, though only my son John is alive now, my twelve grandchildren, twenty-four great-grandchildren and five great-great-grandchildren.

AIR MECHANIC

Henry Allingham

Royal Naval Air Service · *Born* 6 June 1896

I was born in Clapton, east London – back when it was a very good residential area. As a boy, I used to play on the pond with my sailing boat and I was friendly with the sons of Andrews the chemist. They used to have a big house, and I used to go and play with the children there.

It was there that I sat in my first motor car – while the chauffeur was there. I remember they had a lovely orchid house, too, but we could only go in it while the gardener was with us. What I liked best about going there was we used to be given a lovely peach melba in a long glass – and I wasn't used to that sort of thing. They were way ahead of us with their place. There were a lot of lovely swings and roundabouts and nice things in the playroom – and in their garden was a little lake with a boat on that. It was just my cup of tea. I always used to enjoy going there.

At this time I was living with my grandparents, because I lost my father when I was about fourteen months old. I lived with my grandparents until I was seven, and they rather spoiled me. Then I went to live with my mother – she was a very competent person and held a good job.

At the first school I went to there were a lot of rough kids, but I was moved about a lot from school to school. At one of them, I can remember using a box of sand to practise the alphabet. I remember how that box ponged. At another of the schools, one of the boys won the first VC of the war. When we moved to Clapham, my mother wanted to get me into a different, much better school – a London County Council high-grade grammar school in South Lambeth Road. She went to see them and the head said, 'Send the boy up to me and if he can pass the school entrance, I may be able to find a place for him.' So I went to do the exam. He was a lovely man. He put me in the main school hall. He said, 'Now, make haste slowly!' and I did my best and answered all the questions on the paper. And I passed. It was a fantastic school, and they taught us French, science, woodwork, metalwork and art. The art master took us to the Tate Gallery. I used to spend Sunday afternoons at the Tate. I loved that school. I went there until I was almost sixteen and then I came away. We hadn't got much money and were scraping the bottom of the barrel a bit.

My father had been in ironmongery and I was supposed to follow him and enter the family firm – like kids did in those days – but I never wanted to do that. My father's brother, Uncle Dick, was a director of the ironmongery, but I never had much to do with him. My father's other brother, Uncle Will, was the chef at the Bank of England. He was there for some years. When I went to see him there, he'd give me steak and eggs for breakfast. My father's father was a jewel-case maker. He had a factory and employed about eighteen people all the year round. There was a lot of silverware made in those days so there was a lot of call for presentation cases. He was a merry fellow – he always used to wear a red Turkish fez with a black tassel. He used to tease me and play games. He'd pretend to pull my nose off and say, 'Eh, look, you've got your nose in my cup.' I've still got a sovereign case that he made at the factory. It's a marvellous piece of work.

After I left school, my mother couldn't support me and I had to get a job. I went to work at St Bart's Hospital as a trainee surgical instrument maker. I used to get 12/6 a week, and I'd give my mother ten bob and I had half a crown to pay my fares and lunches. Lunch was always meat pud and potato. I began to look like a meat pud. I got my food there Saturdays and Sundays too, but then I chucked that job. They were very, very nice but it wasn't what I wanted to do.

At the same time, I went to evening school at the Regent Street Poly. I did pretty well there. I was always out to learn and I knew what I wanted to do and I knew I had to study to get it.

My next job was at Foden and Scammel, the car-body builder in East Dulwich Road. That was a very high class of work. The first week I thought I was going to get fired but the second week I pulled all the stops out and Albert, the boss, came to me and said, 'You're a good lad. Can you carry on next week? I'll see what I can do for you.' I got 25 bob a week – that was a lot of money for a kid really. I finished up with 29 shillings a week. Well, there were gents going to the city for 30 bob, so I was making a lot of money. I used to be at work at six o'clock in the morning, then I took half an hour for breakfast from eight o'clock to half past. You brought your own breakfast and you were ready for it by then. You had a beer can for your tea. The smithy would fill your can with a measure of water, and you had a whistle of tea and you added milk. At lunchtime the boy used to come round, and he'd go to the shop. You could get steak for 10d, a good steak – and if I was flush I'd have at least twelve ounces of steak. Whoopee! You could braise it on the smithy's fire – he had a grill there – or you could fry it in a pan. You'd get it white hot – I became a master at doing steak – and you'd have lovely fresh oven-baked bread to eat with it. You put it in your toolbox to keep, because if there were any vermin around, they couldn't get in there.

I was on holiday in Brighton with my mother when the war started. After we came home, I wondered what I was going to do. I wanted to go straight into the service, but my mother was on her own and she didn't want that. So I carried on working for a while. Then, in September 1915, my mother died aged just forty-two. As soon as I lost her I joined up.

I went to the RAC in Pall Mall. I had a Triumph TT motorbike at the time and they were looking for dispatch riders for the Royal Engineers. When I told them about my bike, they said they would accept it and that all I had to do was pass the medical. I went along with two others, and they put my name down. I waited. Monday came and still no call and I didn't like that. I wanted them to send for me quickly. I was impatient. One day, I went out for a ride on my pushbike, and I saw an aeroplane and I thought 'That's for me!' The aeroplane belonged to the Royal Naval Air Service at Chingford. I passed the medical at Admiralty Arch, Trafalgar Square. After that, we were given a meal at London Bridge Station and that was lovely.

Then we went to Sheerness where we were trained for a fort-night. I was with fourteen other recruits, including two Aussies, one New Zealander and a Yank – sorry, an American. We were a mixed

Henry Allingham in the uniform of the
Royal Naval Air Service.

lot. When America came into the war in 1917, the Yanks wanted to leave us – but that was fair. They came over to help us and when their own people joined the war, they wanted to be with them. Naturally.

By the second week of training, we were pretty good, and I was asked where I wanted to go. 'Oh, I'll go to East Africa,' I said, but I was sent to Yarmouth instead. Still, there was a lot of action at RNAS Air Station at Great Yarmouth, submarine chasing, for one. I was there for almost two years. That's how it worked: you served two years and then you were posted somewhere else.

At Yarmouth, I came across a very good pilot – Lieutenant Woods. He was known as 'Little Woods' because he was so small. He used to talk to me and this was something, because when you were commissioned, you weren't supposed to speak to the rankers. If they did speak to us we were supposed to stand to attention and blah, blah, blah. Actually, most of the officers didn't like this any more than we did. Some did, though, and a few used to turn the heat on. Anyway Little Woods was very friendly with me and one day he said to me, 'Can you get any good strong rope?' Well, I'd seen plough lines at the local farm, hanging on hooks in a stable, so I said, 'Yes, I may be able to.' So I went up to the stable and got one of the lines that looked new. I took it back and he said, 'Yes, that's it. I want six yards.' So I cut it and gave it to him, and he got in the cockpit of a BE2c and as he sat there, he made me tie him in. They had a belt in the cockpit, and nothing else. I put this rope round the seat and over his shoulders, then I fastened it with a knot and at the back, so he was well fixed in. The only way he could get out was with a knife. 'Righto', he said. I primed the prop for him, and we got the chocks away. He trundled off down the strip and took off. I watched him climbing steeply at an angle. He got halfway up, and I thought he was going to do a tail-slide, but he rocked a bit and over he went. He did three loops – which was quite something in 1915. I met him and undid him when he came down. That evening, he was telling the other fellows what he'd done. He was very pleased with himself.

I remember flying with Egbert Cadbury – the chocolate man. We came down from a night flight and I don't know why, but he knocked the undercarriage away – normally he was a very good pilot. So we made a belly landing, and the consequence was we had to get out of the aircraft really quickly. We got out quick and old Cadbury stood there and really let rip. I thought I'd heard all the swear words in the world, but I learned a whole lot more that day. He was absolutely mad with himself. But I think we'd been very lucky. Cadbury downed two Zeppelins during the war – that was quite something. Leefe Robinson shot one down and got the VC, but Egbert Cadbury got two.

I remember these officers with great affection. I also remember the air station's commanding officer, Lieutenant Commander de Courcy Ireland, and after his death, Lieutenant Commander Douglas Oliver. 'Snakey' Oliver, as he was known, because he was long and sinewy, won the DSO in April 1916, attacking German cruisers that were shelling Great Yarmouth.

Whilst I was at Yarmouth, I was involved in the Battle of Jutland. I was on the armed trawler HMT *Kingfisher* at the time, and I had a Sopwith Schneider seaplane – that was my baby. One Sunday afternoon, my pilot came to fetch me. He told me to get on to the *Kingfisher* so I did. I didn't even have a toothbrush – nothing – but they soon fitted me out and at about four o'clock that Sunday we moved. We had no idea where we were going – but we were going.

On the Monday night, between seven and eight, we were waiting around, when along came the whole Grand Fleet, all in battle line astern, with a big bow wave, going like hell's bells. It was a wonderful sight. The dreadnoughts came first – three of them. Then came the cruisers and everything else right down to the littlest boats, and we joined up with them and followed.

At about 4 o'clock on the Tuesday morning, just before dark lifted, Jerry was spotted. It was really our job in the Schneider to search for Jerry but in the dark we couldn't do very much. So we never flew – we just followed on the rear of the Grand Fleet. While we were there, a lot of dud shells came over, and if those shells had been good I don't think the *Kingfisher* would have fared very well. They either went right over the top or we saw them landing in the water. We heard the noise of the battle – which didn't last too long. The Germans headed away from the British fleet but our people weren't going to fall for that, so instead of going behind them, they went round. I wondered why at the time, but it was because the Jerries were laying mines and if our people had followed them, they would have put them over the side and we would have run into them – and a ship that hit one of those went down, all hands. At the time we didn't really have the sense of being in a major battle. It was only on the following day that we learned what an important battle it had been. In fact, we were completely unaware that it had been a 'victory' until we heard the church bells ringing on the Thursday. I never thought I would live to be the last survivor of the battle.

I met the Schneider pilot ten years later at Turnham Green station – and he was minus one arm. We didn't have any time to speak to each other because we were both in a hurry, so I don't know how he lost it.

When we were flying off the ships, we couldn't stay airborne for long because we'd run out of fuel – that was the trouble. People sometimes had to ditch their aircraft. I saw about seven ditchings. Sometimes the plane would be going up steeply, then it would stop and start going back and it would have no speed – no power. The wind was stronger than the power it had to go forward. In about twelve months they were able to overcome that with a lot more power.

We never ditched – fortunately – because if you ditched you were in big trouble. We never had any parachutes and we didn't have radio. We had pigeons which we carried in a basket – but I never had to use them. Some of our people who were adrift in the drink could be there for up to five days, and they used to let the pigeons go. They would fly back to the loft at the station, and a search party would be sent out to look for them. As a general rule, after five days of searching, they'd give up and the men were lost. However, I met a fellow once who was on leave from the *Halcyon*; he was sitting beside me one afternoon by the River Dee, and he said how he'd been lucky. He'd ditched and they were about to give up looking for him when somebody thought they saw something – and sure enough, it was him. He was very lucky.

In those days you had an open cockpit and it was very cold. You had a leather jacket and a leather helmet, and you'd put Vaseline on your face, and you had gloves to protect you from frostbite. The standard issue was long johns and you had a thick shirt and a vest. Over the top of that you had a grey shirt and a tunic. Your working gear was a tunic with patch pockets, which was very useful and practical. Then you had a choice – you could have trews or you could wear britches and puttees [strips of cloth wound around the leg to form leggings], which took a while to put on. With regard to equipment, you didn't have gun mountings in the aircraft until about June of 1916. That was when we first got the Lewis gun. When I first got in the cockpit, it was my job to sit behind the pilot and defend the plane with two Lee Enfield Rifles.

Once Lewis guns were mounted on our planes, we had the problem of trying to shoot through the propeller. In the air, if you tried it, you'd just shoot the prop away. Then they developed the synchromesh gear with the engine, which synchronised the firing of the machine gun through the prop. It was amazing. We made rapid progress in the last three months of 1916, and from then on we didn't really look back. They gave us the Bristol, Sopwith, Handley Page and so on, and aircraft producers have made good progress from then on. In 1917, they started putting radios in the aircraft. They could send signals over forty miles, so the radio fellows told me, and they could receive signals over sixty. From then on we didn't need the pigeons.

Whilst we were at Yarmouth, we all used to do a bit on the switchboard. Everybody would. I knew that the other fellows would sit there chatting the girls up at the exchange. But I was no chatter-upper – I'd never had a sister – it was all like another nation to me if you like. So I'd go on at seven in the evening and come off at seven in the morning. At about eight o'clock, you'd ring up the exchange and you'd say, 'A time check, please?' And you'd get the time. 'How's the weather there?' All that stuff. I said to one girl who was on there, 'Would you like to hear one of our records?' She said, 'I've heard 'em all.' That shot me down on my first attempt.

In September 1917, we were sent to France to support the Royal Flying Corps. I joined No. 12 Squadron RNAS at Petit Synthe, near

Dunkirk. The squadron had been formed in June 1917 and was equipped with a mixture of Sopwith Pups, Triplanes and Camels. The first thing I did when I got to Calais was to have a nice plate of egg and chips. My job was to service aircraft and to rescue aircraft parts from any machine that crashed behind the lines of trenches. As mechanics, we had to keep the aircraft flying using anything we could. The pilots liked to take their mechanics up in the plane with them, because that way they knew the mechanics would service the plane properly. I used to sit behind the pilot and drop out bombs. If the enemy appeared, I used to open fire with the Lewis gun.

We used to keep more or less with the same pilot, because we became a team. Some of the pilots – you'd hear them come back from flying over the lines and hear some of the stories they used to spin. We had one fellow, Muellock, a Canadian, and he had a Sopwith Triplane with synchronised Lewis guns on board. He did his flying as a loner, and he went over time and time again, but he never had any luck. There was another fellow named Charlie, who used to go over in a group of five – one leading, two on one side and two behind. He was the tail bloke and that made him miserable so he decided to go out alone and he got one the very first time. Yet Muellock tried for months while I was there, and got nothing. That's how it went.

When we moved, we put our gear on lorries – we had fifty-odd lorries and it was very slow going. One lorry would get through and the next one would get stuck in the mud. Then we started joining rubber tyres together and we'd put them down and tow the lorries over them.

Once when we were moving forward on the Ypres Salient to support the offensive, we got to this particular place just as it got dark. It was a strange place and we hadn't been cleared to go forward by the Canadian engineers. There was a lot of fighting in the area and you couldn't walk about as it was too dangerous. It was safest to stay put, so I stuck where I was. I put my groundsheet and blanket down on a bit of concrete and I went to sleep. You didn't have a pillow. You put your boots together and you'd sleep with your head on them. I got up in the night, took a couple of paces and I fell straight into a shell hole. It was absolutely stinking. There was everything in there, you name it – dead rats, no end of rats. You know what they fed on in this hole? The bodies of the boys listed as missing. So there I was, in this filthy great big hole. I decided to take a chance and I moved to the left. If I'd gone to the right, I don't know what would have happened. It was shallow and I managed to get to my feet, and I tried to climb out. I tried several times, but no joy. Somehow though, and I don't know how, I heaved my belly up on to the side, and I could just pull myself out. I was soaking wet, right up to my armpits, but I had to stay where I was until daylight. I didn't dare move again. I wore that kit until it dried off on my body.

We all got lice in our clothes. We used to run the seam of the shirt over a candle flame to get rid of them. Of course, you'd wash your shirt if you could – and when you did wash it, you'd hang it on a bit of line. Next thing you'd see was the lice crawling along the line.

While we were in Flanders, one night, at about half past two, three in the morning, we were shelled from the sea, shelled from the land and bombed from the air all at once. We were caught with our trousers down. Jerry peppered the runway so we couldn't use it. We only had a horse and cart which we used to fill in the holes, but they were fixing something else.

I regretted the fact that we were never given first aid training as on one occasion a pilot landed with a bullet in his thigh, bleeding badly. Although they got him out of the aircraft, he did not survive the journey to the casualty clearing station.

In the Ypres Salient, we used to see the Tommies marching up to and back from the trenches. They came out of the trenches singing 'Take me back to dear old Blighty, put me on a train to London town.' Before we got to Germany, I met some artillerymen who told me that in their battery the guns became red hot from firing, but they couldn't stop. They just kept loading and loading.

On an afternoon off in Belgium, this fellow told me something about a prayer meeting, but he didn't know much more. So I went along to Toc H. The whole area was knocked about a bit but there was a large table alongside a wall, and I walked in and there was Tubby Clayton. He had a big bowl of lovely roses – and seeing them in amongst all these terrible surroundings was really a tear-jerker. Those roses were so beautiful and he was arranging them. He looked at me and said, 'Aren't they lovely? They've just arrived from Blighty this morning.' So I said, 'What's going on here?' He said, 'I've got three men in there, and I'm going to hold communion.' I was ready for communion because I was a full communicant in the Church of England. So I had communion with the other three fellows. Tubby was a very good man. Not only did he help the troops out – he was an army chaplain after all – but it didn't matter who you were: if you were in trouble he'd do his best to sort it out in Blighty for you.

When I got down the line – which wasn't too often – the other fellows would go for beer, but I went for the red wine. For tuppence ha'penny you could have a carafe of lovely *vin rouge* at the estaminet. Louis Freeman (who used to have a timber merchant's in Brighton) was a professional violinist with either the Royal or the

London Philharmonic. When we were at dispersal, he told me that he knew Alfred Cortot, the brilliant pianist, and we used to go down to see him in Dunkirk. When we were there, we could get hold of lots of cans of red salmon. One of those cans was enough for three good meals, so we put a couple of them in our pockets. On one occasion, I remember five of us sharing these tins – myself, Louis Freeman, Alfred Cortot, the Marquis of somewhere or other and Louis Wain, the famous cat artist. I've still got a painting by Wain which he did for me when I was getting married. When I came back to Belgium, he presented it to me. It's a picture of a girl looking out the window and letting the blind up – and she's got no bra on. Typical French. They were good fellows there. We used to share lovely cheese and bread – and plenty of red wine.

The first wine I had was when I was going round possible air-fields with a surveyor. We used to survey places for laying down airfields. We used to go out in the morning, taking our lunch with us, and I used to hold the theodolite up for him while he surveyed the area. Sometimes we'd be all done by 11 o'clock, and then we had the day to ourselves. We'd have a run round the countryside in the Crossley tender, then get back for tea at about five. We used to take our lunch into the estaminet where he could finish his work at the table there and then we had our food and some wine – and there was always coffee after.

March 1918 was the beginning of the end of the war. The Germans made a big push and drove us back, but they ran out of ammo and food, and they were starving and just giving themselves up. A lot of them were herded up into compounds and some went into POW camps. One farmer in England, who had quite a lot of acres, had five of those Germans sent to work for him. He said they never needed supervision: they'd start on the dot, have ten minutes' break in the morning – and ten minutes was ten minutes. He said he could leave them, and they would set the pace, and they would work on steadily. They were good workers and they married local girls, some of them. They didn't go back to Germany.

When the Royal Naval Air Service merged with the RFC to form the RAF on April 1 1918, I was behind St Omer high over the lines. We looked down and we could see the line, right the way round. Trenchard, who was boss of the RAF, thought he was going to have all the air resources but the Admiralty wouldn't have that, of course. We navy fellows had about nine months when we didn't know what we were, really, RN or RAF. There was a bit of argument, but we were eventually merged into the RAF.

When the war ended I was in Belgium. Naturally, everybody went mad – but I didn't. I took to my bed and had a good night's sleep. There were a good many men who never saw the morning because they all went crazy. If they had a rifle and bullets, they'd shoot, just to make a noise. The Very* lights went up all around, and people went crazy. I wasn't going to do that. I thought I'd get a good sleep while I could. When the rest came in the morning they were all over the place – but I was allright. We were supposed to move at eight o'clock but we didn't get away until eleven, because chaps were coming in in dribs and drabs. Then we got under way and we went through Belgium and into Germany, to the Rhine, and I got to Cologne. I remember going into the hotel opposite the cathedral. I spoke to the chef, who had worked in London for eight years before the war. He offered me something to eat; it was black and a bit smaller than an Oxo cube. Goodness knows what it was but it gave me

---

* Very lights were a standard type of coloured flare fired from a pistol.

indigestion for two hours afterwards. Just after Christmas, Dorothy sent me two lovely oranges. By today's value they were like platinum. Where she got those from I never knew.

Dorothy and I had met at Yarmouth when she was a nurse and I was in hospital with a cracked rib. I married her in late 1918. In fact, I never wanted to get married at the time but in the middle of 1918 I was sent for when I was at dispersal and told, 'There's a commission for you.' I was all for it, but I wanted to think about it at home. I was given four days' special leave to make my decision. I got a destroyer from Dunkirk over to Dover. When I told Dorothy what I was going to do, she burst into tears. She wouldn't have that – there was a very high rate of casualty. And she said, 'You've got no home (which I didn't have) and it's time you thought about settling down.' I turned to her, and I said, 'Would you marry me?' She was stunned. I'd never intended to do that – I didn't want to get married. And she said 'Oh! Yes.' And that was that.

I remember a nice joke from the time that shows you what we thought of generals. This fellow was going on the *Royal Scot* from Euston to Edinburgh, and he hadn't booked a seat. He walked along the platform looking for a corner seat and saw one – but there were already three men in there. He asked them if it was taken and they said hop in. So he got in and one man started speaking as the train moved off. He said, 'Well gentlemen, we've got a long way to go. We should introduce ourselves.' He carried on, 'I'm an army general and I'm happily married,' and the second fellow said, 'Strange, I too am a general,' and the third one said, 'So am I,' so the little bloke in the corner says, 'I'm a sergeant major – and I've got three illegitimate sons, and they're all generals.'

After the war my first job was with an aircraft company and I was on £4 a week. That wasn't bad because it was ten bob over the average. It was good money for 1919, but after a time I knew that I could do better, and I turned that job in. The next one I had, I was paid for the job I did, and I made good money that way. I went from £4 a week to £16 a week. I said to Dorothy, 'It won't always be like this, so you'd better put some by,' and of course she used to save some money out of that.

After that, I had a good job at Price's of Edinburgh [an engineering firm] for twelve years. For the first twelve months, it was terrible, but after that I could do no wrong. And every day there was something fresh.

During the Second World War, I worked on a number of military projects. One of them was trying to find counter-measures to German magnetic mines. In fact, one year I was sitting down to my Christmas dinner, when there was a ring at the bell. It was someone calling me down to the plant. I said, 'Well, get yourself a drink, and I'll be down.' I'd got my own transport – I did right through the war – and I said I'd be there soon. I finished my lunch and left my wife and two daughters and went to the plant – and I didn't see my bed for eight nights after that. What had happened, a lot of magnetic mines had been dropped near Biggin Hill. We had to devise something to get rid of those mines. We managed to do it. They used our method to clear the mines blocking Harwich. In due course every ship that was built had this device to neutralise magnetic mines. Even after the war, they still put them in there.

Dorothy and I were married for almost fifty-three years before she died in 1970. We had two daughters – June died in 2001, aged seventy-eight. She married an American airman in the last war and went to America. That's where my five grandchildren and twelve great-grandchildren live. Betty, our other daughter, lost touch a long time ago.

Thinking back to the first war, I don't think I knew what to expect. I thought we'd win – but I never thought we'd have to fight again like that for a hundred years. I'll never forget my comrades, but you can't dwell on the terrible things that happened. You couldn't go on if you did. But on days like Armistice Day, I pray for them. At the Cenotaph in 2004 I was thinking of the blokes I knew who burned. I saw them come down – men I knew, whose planes I knew – crashing into the ground.

There's good stuff to remember: the camaraderie and knowing you can depend on your mate, but not the other things. I used not to think about it at all, but now people want to talk to me about it because I'm one of the few left. So now I have to think more about it. But there are things I would rather not think about. In fact it often feels like something that happened to someone else.

On my hundred and ninth birthday, I was taken out for lunch in Eastbourne by Dennis Goodwin, the President of the World War I Veterans' Association, who has looked after me for many years. I received a great number of cards and was particularly pleased with the card from the Queen. The RAF and navy sent a senior officer, who both gave me a souvenir recalling my time with the RNAS and the RAF. Especially moving for me was to receive a gift from young Tom from Ardingly College whose ninth birthday it was. It was amazing to think that there are a hundred years between us.

There's a lot that I've tried hard to forget – but I've got a lot to be thankful for. I'm still here. I've had a unique sort of life. I've scraped the barrel and I've had the cream.

Cecil Withers

17th Battalion Royal Fusiliers · *Born* 9 June 1898, *died* 17 April 2005

I was born on 9 June 1898 in Rotherhithe. I had four sisters – Florence, who lived to be over a hundred; next was Gwennie who lived 'til she was ninety, and Ruby, who was my twin. She was a very talented pianist, but she died in 1920 from TB. Finally there was Gladys, who was killed with her husband in August 1944 by a flying bomb when they were both on duty as ARP wardens. I had a brother, Bert, about three years older than me, who died during the First World War. He was a very nice boy. He wasn't in the army. He was too weak, and he died of consumption. My other older brother, Arthur, who later became head of a rope manufacturer in east London, was in the artillery and survived the war. My mum was worried at us two boys being away. There was a lot of worry in those days amongst the families – she had lost my little brother Douglas when he was about seven. He was ill and was left in his bedroom, but was found later wandering around in ice-cold conditions in only a nightshirt, and he died of bronchitis.

I was five when I went to school and I stayed until about thirteen. After that, I went to work for WH Smith and Sons, where I was a bookkeeper. I worked in the office of the General Manager, Mr William Smart, in Arundel House in the Strand, opposite the Law Courts. I had to wear a collar with studs, and a tie. Every morning, I used to take the Number 74 tram from Brockley, which only took about twenty-five minutes to get to the office – which was quite fast in those days. In the thirties it was about forty minutes. Sometimes the tram would stop because a horse had gone down ahead. A 'bloody horse' had slipped on the cobbles and caused a stoppage. When that happened, sacks were laid all around so the horse could gain a footing on the road surface.

When the war broke out in 1914, I was at camp with the Scouts at St Mary Cray Woods. Our scoutmaster, Mr C. Everard Jay, joined up straight away and was killed at Mons. In December 1915, when I was seventeen and a half, I ran away from home to join the 4th Battalion, East Surreys. I was under age so I had to lie to the recruiting sergeant. I said I was eighteen years old and my name was Sydney Harrison. If I hadn't, my father would have got them to send me back home and that would have been humiliating. I told the truth later, though, because if I'd been killed as Harrison, nobody would ever have known what had happened to me. After I came clean, I was on parade and the sergeant shouted, 'Private Withers, two paces forward. Harrison yesterday, Withers today, when was the bloody wedding then?'

I trained in Cornwall for more than six months and I learned to use the Lee Enfield .303 and the Lewis gun. We finally arrived in France at the end of 1916. My first action was at the Battle of Arras on Easter Sunday, 1917. As we approached the trenches, we walked through a churchyard and the first thing I saw was a foot and a leg sticking out of the soil. That was a nasty introduction. Very alarming. It was snowing at the time and I'll tell you another thing – it was so cold that when you went to take a drink from your water bottle you got nothing. It had turned to ice.

Arras was the first time I went over the top. We played football together as we went over. That was the tradition in the East Surreys. I remember the ball dropping at my feet and I passed it to Captain Maxwell. 'That was a good pass you made, young Withers!' he shouted before he thumped it towards the German lines.

I got wounded at the end of that battle. I was temporarily blinded in one eye but it could have been worse. At the end of the battle, I lay bleeding in a trench. There was blood coming out of my eye, pouring out all over my face. My head looked blown in. They thought I was dead and they were going to bury me. I was in a half-conscious state and I can remember a soldier getting hold of me and saying, 'Here – this bloke's alive!' That man saved my life, by calling that out. I'd have been buried alive in Arras, if it hadn't been for him.

After being wounded, I came back to Solihull in Birmingham and was in hospital for about a month, and then they sent me down to Cornwall to a convalescent camp. When I got out of there, I was transferred from the East Surreys to the 17th Battalion Royal Fusiliers and I stayed with them until the end.

I think we had a few days' leave at Christmas time, 1917. I received a telegram saying that leave was extended until Sunday midnight for the expeditionary force. A few days later I had to report to Felixstowe and was sent straight back to France to the trenches again where I stayed from January to November 1918. I was there for the Second Battle of the Somme in March 1918. That was the toughest fighting I went through. I remember going out into no-man's-land one day, and seeing a poor German soldier, half dead. He was calling out, *'Wasser, Wasser!'* And I got out my water bottle and gave it him to drink. He was so terribly grateful. The way he looked at me was so moving. That's always stayed with me.

On another day, I went out with some stretcher bearers. We saw one wounded man and the sergeant said, 'Withers, get that man to the casualty clearing station.' I put my rifle down but the sergeant said, 'You must keep your rifle – don't you leave it.' So I put the man over my shoulder and went off to find the casualty clearing station. As I came to a set of crossroads, a couple of officers went by on horse-back. They looked at me and said, 'Where's your rifle?' I thought what a bunch of lousy bastards. If I'd not had that rifle, they'd have assumed that I was a deserter and had just slung a dead body over my shoulder and I'd have been shot. Luckily for me I was carrying my rifle. The man I was carrying was badly wounded. I never said a word to him. I didn't even know who he was. When I got to the casualty clearing station, they took him off my shoulder and put me on a stretcher. They gave me a dose of smelling salts, and said maybe I should have a bit of rest, so I lay there and I dozed off. When I woke up, I had to find my way back to my unit. I was walking along in no-man's-land until I came to some troops from some regiment or other. 'Can you tell me where the Fusiliers are?' I asked. 'Oh yes, they're way down in that direction.' So off I went. But all the time I was going back I kept thinking of that poor boy and what happened to him.

One night we were at the front and this man and I were talking. He got out a photo of a little girl. He said she was his little sister. 'She prays for me every night,' he said. Just moments later a shell burst near us, and a splinter of shrapnel went straight into his brain. He'd told me earlier that if anything happened to him, I must write to his mother and say that he died instantly. But I didn't even know his name – I only knew he was from Leamington Spa. Everyone used to say the same thing, though. They asked anyone who survived to tell their mum, 'he died instantly'. They wouldn't have wanted them to know some of the things I saw and heard. You wouldn't believe the terrible moaning and crying of the poor boys who were wounded, calling out, 'Mum, Mum!' It breaks my heart to think of it. Their suffering was terrible.

There was gas. I suffer badly from phlegm and from coughs and colds a lot. That all started when the British were shelling hard at the last Battle of the Somme. One of the shells disturbed the residue of mustard gas that had been lying there for months. They talk about secondary smoking . . . I got secondary gas. It really hit me for six.

I remember a few of us standing around, holding on to each other's shoulder out of sheer exhaustion. It was so bitterly cold and there was no food, no hot drinks. Nothing. Suddenly, we all dropped. The officers looked at us and said, 'Let them stay where they are.' So nobody worried us until we were able to get up. I was taken away and treated behind the lines for three weeks. After that, I was back to the front again.

One problem we had was the lice. Terrible things, they were. Terrible little transparent things that went black when they were full of blood. When we were in the trenches, we used to take a little candle with us, and when it was quiet, we'd sit out on the firesteps, light the candle and pass the seams of our trousers over the flame so that all the little lice were burned. The lice popped as they went over the candle flame. The worst thing was when you got lice in the middle of your back. I used to get my bayonet out, and pass it over my shirt. It was the only way to get rid of them. Then there were the cockroaches – they were terrible stinking things. They fed on the dead who were lying out beyond our reach. We couldn't lay them to rest.

I remember the food. Mostly we had Fray Bentos corned beef and dog biscuits, as we used to call them. They were terribly hard so you had to soften them with water. And there was Maconochie's stew maybe once a month. We got some bread sometimes – and water, and what they called tea for breakfast, lunch and supper. In the reserve we used to get to sit down at a table, but the food was just the same as in the trenches.

The *Daily Mail* used to send two-pound tins of Christmas pudding for us at the front. They sent them every Christmas, and the officers would wait on the men for their Christmas dinner. Everyone had a portion of Christmas pudding – everyone had their share from a two-pound tin.

Sometimes there were concert parties for a bit of entertainment and sometimes the band would play marches. There was one march I used to love, 'Old Comrades' – even though it was a German march by Carl Teike. It was a lovely march that was. It reminded me of when we were training in Cornwall and all the kiddies would follow behind us when we marched.

As 1918 went on, we were advancing and we began to feel that we were winning. When we overran the German lines, there were all sorts of comforts in the dugouts. They had samovars with hot coffee and drinks and straw paliasses laid out on the ground. But we had to stop in the trench all night. We always slept in the trench. We used to dig a place for ourselves and curl up and go to sleep or sit on the bloody steps leading down into the dugout and try to sleep there. Our people treated us like dogs. They were cruel bastards compared with the Germans. I remember a major from the East Surreys. In any conditions, he used to get us out on parade, march us up and down. He was a rotten swine. Eventually we heard that somebody shot him. That sort of thing could happen.

The worst moment I can recall was when we were advancing, and we got to a point by the St Quentin canal. I was standing in front of the canal, and there was a queue waiting to cross over to the other side. The man in front of me stepped forward, and as he did so, a shell burst over his head and he looked like a concertina collapsing. It killed him stone dead in front of me and the blast threw me back on those who were following. Then I had to cross this rickety bridge with all these machine guns firing at me all the time. But somehow I got safely to the other side without being hit or knocked off. If you fell in the water, no one could have saved you. I was loaded with heavy equipment and I'd have sunk without a trace.

After that, we went marching on, following the Germans as they retreated. They were retreating faster than we could follow them. You couldn't see their horses for dust, they were going that quick. As we passed through towns and villages, the French girls used to sing a song: *'Après la guerre finit, soldats anglais partent,'* ['The war having finished, the English soldiers will leave.'] to the tune of *'Sur les ponts de Paris'*. They used to say: *'Anglais soldats tres bons – Allemands soldats pas bons'* [English soldiers very good – Germans soldiers not good]. At the time of the Armistice, I was in Le Treport and nobody took much notice because people were still getting killed by booby traps and we didn't feel the war was over.

When it was all finished, I was in the Army of Occupation. We went into Cologne and I remember hearing the music in the cafés. There were plenty of cafés in Germany. In the Hochstrasse in Cologne, there were three or four lovely cafés. These places had a string orchestra, with violins and cellos. All we'd had was a squeeze box to listen to. What a contrast.

After that, I was sent to Cornwall, where I put my name down to go into boxing. Our boxing instructor was the heavyweight champion Sergeant Major 'Bombardier' Billy Wells from the Fusiliers. I put the gloves on with him, and he said, 'Go on, Withers, try and hit me.' I said, 'If I hurt you, it will be your fault! You told me to do it!' He laughed – and the others laughed too. I couldn't get a punch in because he'd parry each one. Then he landed one on me. One punch, down I went and they carried me out on a stretcher. I was unconscious for several hours. The doctors were worried about me. I think I've been affected by that ever since – that blow to the head. Several years ago, I sat down and couldn't get up. I was temporarily paralysed and I went to Queen Mary's Hospital but it was nothing permanent. After a few days it eased off. A couple of years afterwards I was dropped down again with paralysis of the neck. It was all brought on by that shock to the brain from the boxing.

Some years after the war was over I was walking past County Hall, and I was going down the steps when I passed a man who looked at me and said, 'Hello, Withers, what are you doing here?' I looked up and recognised Captain Maxwell – the officer I played football with as I went over the top at Arras. I told him that I was looking for a job and he said he'd be pleased to help me and that I should go to see a Major Bowen. Thanks to him, I started work as a clerk in the Ministry of Food, in Palace Chambers, opposite Big

Ben. After it was dissolved, I went to the Inland Revenue. I retired from there in 1963.

I married my wife, Gracie Bourne, as soon as the war was finished. We had two sons. My eldest son was an RAF pilot in the Second World War. He was a flight sergeant but we lost him in 1944 over the Aegean Sea. We had evacuated from London to Llandudno, and I was in my office, sitting at my desk, when I received the telegram telling me that he was dead. He was just twenty-four.

After the war, I decided to learn comparative religion so I went to the Christopher Humphries Library to study. Christopher Humphries was head of the Buddhist League, and he had a little private library. I went there one day and he said to me, 'OK, Mr Withers, don't you bother to ring any more – I'll show you how to get in.' He showed me where there was a lever behind the back door – and how to press it to make the door open. So I got to come and go without knocking. I was studying for personal reasons. For all the suffering and death I saw in the trenches, I never lost my faith. I still pray and I still believe.

The fact that I'm still here is because of some power above. There's no doubt about it. Divine help. In 1986, I went to Queen Mary's Hospital and had three major operations. I had peritonitis, a duodenal ulcer and a hernia. I had those three operations on the trot, one after another, and Mr Hamlyn the surgeon said, 'You're the first one I've ever had that's gone through all these operations and come out the other side.' I was only eighty-eight then. After that I find it hard to believe that I outlived my dear twin sister by eighty-five years.

I went and saw the play *Journey's End* a few years ago. It was on at a theatre in the Strand. I remember watching one of the characters sitting in the dugout, shooting at a rat. I identified with that character.

That's what it was like and it's important that people know what it was like. I remember once, on the Somme, seeing half a dozen of our English boys, all in pieces in a big shell hole. They were half buried, stinking. It was hot and there was a terrible stench and they were covered in bluebottles and cockroaches. It was a terrible sight. Those poor boys. It made me sick. We had to smoke strong Turkish cigarettes to hide the smell. On the firestep in the trenches during the night, you could hear the groaning of the dying – but you couldn't could go out to help them. There were rats feeding on their flesh. They were lying there, dying in pain and misery, and the rats were nibbling away at their flesh. Cockroaches did that as well, they fed on their blood.

People still talk a lot of rubbish about the war. I've always let people know what really went on. I suppose I was breaking the rules. I've let people know so that the truth could be a warning to them. When the war was going on, its horrors were kept quiet and the full display of dreadful things only came out afterwards. These things were carefully hidden at the time. There was wartime censorship and the most gruesome things were concealed. These days, if any trigger-happy politician wants to start another war, it's my job to let people know what that means. Politicians today are pitiless humbugs. What do they know? Only those who were there can tell what really happened. Tell of the suffering and misery.

Alfred Finnigan

Royal Field Artillery · *Born* 18 September 1896, *died* 11 May 2005

I was born in London – Deptford in fact, the dockyard of the British navy in the reign of Henry VIII. My father was the third son of Mr Brian Bernard Finnigan of Manchester, who had established a flourishing business there, and my father, I have to confess, was not competent. He wasn't mad or anything of that type, but let's be quite frank – my father was a fool. He got it into his head as a young man to go to Australia. Luckily for him, he was left sufficient money to keep going without any trouble; in fact he misused the money. He did all right with it; he eventually took his wife and little me to Australia in 1903, where there was nothing to do, but he'd got it into his thick head that Australia was a good place – but it wasn't. He opened various establishments before settling into the old family trade of making travel goods, such as suitcases and trunks. Following the birth of my younger brother, the whole family had to return to England due to the poor health of my brother. He was born with an enlarged heart and the climate in Australia was too hot for him.

On returning to England, my father found it difficult to find any suitable permanent work and when he died, he was lucky that the money had lasted just long enough. Nevertheless, it was a foolish life.

He was an influence in so far as he introduced me to the delights of reading and to Gilbert and Sullivan – they were the few nice things my father did. Gilbert and Sullivan I liked very much, and still do. My father used to take me to the theatre whenever a Gilbert and Sullivan production opened in Melbourne.

I was six when I went to Australia, and I stayed there until I was about ten. Then we came back to England, back to Tottenham. I went to a Catholic school – why, heaven only knows, because I should have gone back to my original school in Tottenham, which was an ordinary school with no pretensions at all – Tottenham School. I should have just gone back to the class I left.

Deep down I wanted to live in St John's Wood so I could watch the cricket at Lords or get the tube to the Oval. My father took me to see the fifth test match at Lords in 1909 – England and Australia. One of the Australians was Ponsford – and it was a draw. I've always enjoyed cricket.

I don't think the country in general had any appreciation of the war. It's one thing I learned as a young man that the war – like all wars – was an idiotic thing. Absolutely idiotic, and I didn't enjoy my elders supporting the whole damn thing. But I tried to join up following Kitchener's appeal, but was turned down because I was only five foot three, and I had an eye weakness. I finally joined up at Kennington, near the Oval – it would be 21 September 1914. I joined the 2/6 [2nd Battalion, 6th Regiment] Royal Field Artillery, 13th Battery as a driver – but I didn't leave London for a year. I trained

Alfred Finnigan in the uniform of the
Royal Field Artillery.

in London and Hertfordshire – we were in the barracks in Hyde Park – where a horse bit me in the chest. It was funny. I went round to the hospital in Praed Street; they poked me about a bit – which was as painful as the bite. We went down to Wiltshire for final training and it was a good camp – a damn good camp, and we did well there. I was lead driver of a gun team; it took three drivers to control the six horses who pulled the guns.

Eventually we went to Southampton and to France from there. We landed at Le Havre and we put in two or three days there under canvas, and then we went up to the line. I remember being shipped on because they were bombing Le Havre.

We arrived in the Somme area at the end of that campaign and were in action in the Béthune, La Bassée area. Our gun positions here were a little to the west of Cuinchy on the south side of the La Bassée Canal. At La Bassée I was detailed to pick up a gun from a position in the 'Swampy Woods' area to the west of a place called Windy Corner. It was in the middle of the night when it was much safer for any movement. Well, we got the gun limbered up and made for the canal bank, but it was a damned dark night – the team was pulling hard and I just saw the gleam of the canal water in time to avoid it. The route took us along the canal bank, over the bridge at Pont Fixe through the ruins of Cuinchy and Cambrai and on to Division at Béthune.

Winter was terrible for both us and the horses – I can only say the conditions were dreadful. Freezing cold weather and snow – it was simply dreadful. I cannot describe it, how the poor horses suffered. We had the chance of getting some Canadian knee-length boots which were much better than ours. I don't know what came over me, but I chose a pair of size tens – and I only wore sevens. It

Alfred Finnigan, hatless and in shirtsleeves to the left of centre.

was the best choice I ever made. Like the other chaps, I rubbed grease – any kind of grease would do – all over my feet, and covered them with two pairs of thick woollen army socks. Then I stuffed clean hay into the boots and laced them on. Ahh – but they were warm! Our hands were always frozen. Gloves didn't last long as the traces just wore them away. Over our heads we wore balaclavas – and a bit of straw under our tin hats helped keep the cold away. Around our necks we had woollen mufflers, then greatcoats covered with groundsheets. These groundsheets reached over the horses' hindquarters and kept us both reasonably dry. I don't know what I looked like, but I can only describe myself as a 'military vagabond'. But the weather was just snow, sleet and ice – it was indescribable. Our food was not too good either, and we used to complain. This would prompt an order from GHQ. Once, when we complained about the quality of the pork-and-beans ration, the order stated, 'On opening a tin of pork and beans, soldiers must not be disappointed if they find no pork. The pork has been absorbed into the beans.' One soldier wrote back asking if it would be safe to transport beans and bully beef in the same lorry, in case the bully beef would be absorbed in the same way!

We moved to the Vimy front in the spring of 1917. Our base was near the village of Neuville-St-Vast. Here I wrote in my diary:

Passchendaele 29 March
The weather was awful. Rain, hail, much snow and cold winds. The horses stood nearly to their hocks in mud, many dying through the hard work and exposure, some having to be shot. The sufferings of the drivers this month alone would take a long time in telling.

In blustery wind, rain, sleet and snow, the attack began at 5.30 on 9 April. The attack was aimed at Thelus Trench and Goulot Wood, and the job of the 18-pounders was to cut the wire that might hold up the assaulting troops. We had to approach further forward in order to hit the target – and this before our own infantry attacked, so we were open to attack from artillery and infantry fire, as well as being vulnerable to friendly fire from the big guns in the rear. Our entire battery was caught on the curve on one side of the ridge. Men were lying all over the road. We had packhorses, and a 5.9 shell landed beside me at the top of the ridge. All I got was earth on my tin hat, but men and horses before and behind me got hit. There was a team blasted against the bank, the lead driver still in his saddle, his right leg off at the knee. However, by 2 p.m. that day, the entire ridge, with two small exceptions, was taken. Later that evening I wrote in my diary:

9 April

Battery took part in capture of Vimy Ridge by Canadian Corps. Remained in action covering the front until the night of the 14th. My own battery pulled out from Neuville-St-Vast at dusk after working all day. I was lead driver of leading gun with eight horses in the team near the recent front lines and no-man's-land.

We stuck in the thick mud. Three times myself and my horses were brought down as we struggled to get the gun out. Very dark.

Ammunition was brought up by pack. Hedges and Dr Sparvel were wounded and eighteen horses killed, wounded and missing, the area being heavily shelled all night.

Alfred Finnigan, left and hatless.

On 16 April, we came under a gas-shell attack. The team ahead of me put gas masks on and finished up in a ditch. It was a very dark night and I just put on nose clips and mouthpiece, leaving my eyes clear. I got gassed, but we all got through, and my eyes soon cleared. We reported the incident as soon as we got back, and the MO went out to see if he could do anything for the men. During that spring and summer we seemed always to be on the move and in action. I recorded some of the moments in my diary:

16 April

We lived and worked in great misery, unable often to get a wash or shave, and when we did, only in great discomfort.

Infected with vermin and hardly any sleep. A shell burst alongside me but I was unhurt.

The road on the Ridge was littered with wrecked guns, wagons and dead and dying horses and men. An awful smell hung over this land.

23 April

In the early morning the enemy shelled the battery with gas shell persistently until dawn. Sergeant Rodgers was hit in the shoulder by a shrapnel bullet and evacuated. Sergeant Gibson was hit in the side and shoulder as he rode beside me.

The gas shelling was a bit of a nuisance while driving. The tear gas shell half blinding me, which usually meant finishing up in the ditch. I used my rubber mouthpiece and nose clips in case there was any poison gas mixed with it.

29 April

At 11.15 a.m. a whizz-bang fell in the mess, wounding Major Gilman so seriously that he died without recovering consciousness.

30 April

There has been a rolling barrage of gas attack.

3 May

All objectives taken after very heavy fighting and large casualties. 2 British Division took Affrey, but failed to hold it. They were very badly hammered. Roeux taken. A dump was set on fire in rear of number 6 gun by a shell during an SOS. Staff Sergeant Maynard, Corporal Grey, Gunner Burrows and Thompson most gallantly threw earth on it and beat it with bags. All recommended MMs (Military Medals). The weather turned to quite warm. It was like heaven.

4 June

We are badly knocked about. Trenches very wet and muddy. Major Bolster MC killed while taking ammunition up to the guns. Another brave gentleman lost.

11 July

King George came down at 10 a.m. to inspect the battalion of 63 Division on polo ground. One hundred men from 15 Brigade formed a party on side of road. After two hours waiting they only managed a very feeble cheer. A very sad stunt.

22 July

Hun aircraft very active. Reconnoitred our back areas at least twice during day.

During a night move on the Lens–Arras road our gun got stuck in the mud and the team was unable to move it. They added another two horses and then another two joined the team, and eventually ten horses were used to get it out.

In late September the artillery moved to the village of Habarcq, and they held a race meeting. Also, while we were there, the 5 Division concert troupe, 'The Whizz-Bangs', put on a show – that was the only entertainment of the war that I saw.

18 September

At Habarcq I found it very pleasant after the bareness of the Vimy Front. It is quite a pretty place with a stream running near the horse lines, which was very convenient. I had my 21st birthday, receiving some very nice presents from home and my friends.

Frank, my wheel driver, was on leave and returned just before we left. We got a great many apples here from an orchard and they came in very useful on the march to supplement the grub, which was never enough.

22 September

Very fatiguing night march to Polincove, going to sleep in the saddle. Weather very warm. Although we had billets, some of us slept in the open. Frank, Fred Smith and I slept under a hedge.

It was most enjoyable and healthy. It was Fred's last bit of pleasure under the sun and fresh wind – he was killed at Ypres, buried hastily near the guns.

His body was blown up a few days after and scattered about over the mud and slime. He was a jolly fine fellow and was my very good friend. I hope if there's another and better world that he is there. He's well earned it.

During the Ypres campaign I had to drive between the ammunition dump at Zillebeke and our gun teams on the northern lip of the Hooge Crater. Both routes through the area involved using the Menin Road, which was a straight line from the eastern outskirts of Ypres. There were two junctions which were well known hot-spots – Hellfire Corner and Halfway House. Once at Hellfire Corner, I had been returning from Hooge when my leading offside horse shied from a shell explosion and slipped into a crater. We tried everything to pull him out, all the time under shell fire, but it seemed hopeless. We must have been fifteen minutes struggling like mad, knowing we could all be killed any moment. He was a great favourite of mine, but he was 'windy', and no use as an army mount. He should never have been in the army. He was screaming and thrashing about so much that I finally decided there was nothing else for it but to shoot him and cut the traces. It was then that, suddenly and with no reason, he broke free and out he came.

On another occasion I was cleaning out the stables when one of my favourite horses got a bit fractious and, getting impatient, I gave him a smack with a broom handle. It would have been all over and done with if the captain hadn't seen it, and put me on a report. I couldn't believe it. He crimed me. He crimed me for the only time I ever hit my horse.

Alfred Finnigan, far left, at the stable
with horses and other riders.

30 September

There is no need to go into detail about describing Ypres. We lost all six guns in turn and had very heavy casualties.

I lost my Sergeant, Corporal and two Bombardiers, several gunners killed and wounded, one driver wounded and several sick as it was ammunition carrying day and night. Everything was mud and water and continuous shelling. Hell with the lid off.

Depending on the weather, the Hooge Crater could be bone dry, a morass or a lake – but usually a morass. In October 1917, it was muddy and slippery and a battery of 18-pounder guns was in position close to the eastern lip where we were servicing them. I had to take my team through the crater and weave very carefully through the many casualties lying there on stretchers. I made it through without running over any of them, but it's not an easy task to take a gun limber through mud. The horses were very good and wouldn't step on anyone if they could avoid them. It was also here that our battery lost all six of its guns from enemy fire.

8 October

The road was a very hot shop all the time and having finished carrying ammo up, usually three loads with two packhorses, a man got out of this place as quickly as his horse could take him.

The closest I ever came to being shot was at Zillebeke, when I was chatting to a pal during a lull. We heard a 'ziiip' noise and we knew that a bullet had whizzed between our heads. We dived to the ground but we never knew if we were the target or whether it was just a stray shot.

At the end of 1917, we were moved to Italy. The train journey lasted five days and it was an absolute joy to see the Mediterranean and see the sun shining. The morale of the Italian army was low, and it had been pushed back from the Osonzo Front to the mountains beyond the Piave River. One night, north of the village of Arcade, our team saw an enemy aircraft and we realised we were his target. I drove the team into the deep black shadow of a roadside shrine and watched as the pilot released his bombs. We were unscathed.

When Haig gave his 'Backs to the Wall' order, in April 1918, we were sent back to the Western Front, to the River Lys, between Nieppe Forest and St Venant. After travelling fifty miles from Doullens we went straight into action, swinging our guns through the hedgerows. We moved into a field, along by the hedges where, here, it was the first time I received an order as in training: 'HALT! ACTION RIGHT!' The gunners unlimbered, swung their guns to the hedges and began to register. Our lines were between the orchard trees. That night was quite quiet, but at 10 o'clock the next morning the Germans launched their attack, beginning with a heavy bombardment. We repulsed each of their four attacks with good infantry and artillery work – we sweated our horses black, up and down from Division, field to guns with ammo all day. It was gruelling work on a hard road in fine weather. Two and a quarter million rounds of small arms ammunition was sent up to replace what was expended.

We learned that the Armistice had been signed while we were on the Pont-sur-Sambre, and after that we remained at Le Quesnoy until 13 December, when we went into billets near Namur. I spent another five months assisting with demobilisation and then came home in 1919 and was demobbed in May.

The prospect of secure employment looked bleak in the mass

unemployment that followed the end of the war – so I decided to return to Australia to seek my fortune. However, conditions were just as bad in Australia, and after some seven years of doing odd jobs 'up country', around Mildurra and Red Cliffs, north-west of Melbourne, I finally signed up as a deckhand on 31 March 1927 to work my passage home on the *William Mitchell*. Ordinarily this would not be particularly noteworthy, however, what made it extraordinary was the fact that the *William Mitchell* was a fully rigged three-masted ship, transporting cargo all over the world. In fact, this is believed to have been the last voyage of a fully rigged sailing ship flying the British flag.

The voyage started from Melbourne, and went on to Callao in Peru, then to Tocopilla, and finally to Ostend, via the Panama Canal, where I was discharged on 27 November 1927, earning my seaman's ticket in the process. At some point in the South Pacific Ocean, I was nearly washed overboard during a typhoon, but was able to grab hold of the rope that runs the length of the ship down both sides. I then managed to swing myself back on board as the ship rolled back, and continued to carry out the orders I had been given. I am quite philosophical about the whole matter – it was just 'one of those things'. At the end of the voyage the ship was broken up for salvage – that was a sad day for me as I returned to London.

I undertook a number of jobs until the outbreak of World War Two. Initially hired as a fire-watcher for the printers Blades, East and Blades in the City, I was soon made assistant cashier due to the holder of that post being called up to the services, and I remained there until my retirement in 1961.

When I married I made a conscious decision that we should not have children – I was not prepared to produce cannon fodder for the army, nor fodder for industry.

These days I've got no time for governments and politicians – or for any form of religion. None of these emerged from the Great War with flying colours. Lessons have gone unheeded and mankind keeps on repeating its mistakes. I refuse to watch television because of the war, bad news and rubbish it features. I recently had a minor eye operation, and this has restored my sight so I can enjoy reading my books again. I'd rather cut myself off from what goes on in the world today. The First World War was idiotic. It started out idiotic and it stayed idiotic. It was damned silly, all of it.

Fred Lloyd

Royal Field Artillery · *Born* 23 February 1898, *died* 28 April 2005

I was born on 23 February 1898 at Copwood in Uckfield. One hundred and six years later, I'm still in the same town. I like it here.

There were sixteen of us in our family – I had eight sisters and seven brothers. My parents really loved children. I was the last one to be born, and I'm the only one left alive. My mother died when she was forty-three – I learned from one of my sisters that she died in childbirth. My father died soon after and they said it was from a broken heart. One of my sisters died young – she was also forty-three – and two of my brothers were killed in the first war – Thomas and William. Thomas was thirty-two when he died. William was only twenty-two when he was killed. He was a giant – six foot four – and he joined up on the day war broke out when he'd only just turned eighteen. He was with the 1st Battalion, Scots Guards. There were four of us who joined up. Only two came home.

I was five years old when I started at Holy Cross School – it's still there but the actual building is now the Holy Cross Church Centre.

That school celebrates its 155th birthday in 2005 – I think I am its oldest surviving pupil! There were fifty children in the class – all of us five years old. I remember the first day: Emily, my sister, was crying and one of the little girls wet herself, and it ran all along the floor. That was a hundred years ago.

I used to walk over a mile to school with my brothers and sisters. The school day started at nine and at twelve we had a break. Then we carried on until four. In the break, we played conkers, skipping and football – except we used to kick a tennis ball because we didn't have a proper football. We played marbles as well – they say you lose your marbles, but I haven't lost mine. Well, not yet. I was pretty good most of the time, but the headmaster, Mr Richard, used the stick on me once. I let a firework off in the cloakroom and it went off right outside his window. When he gave you the stick, he liked to hit you on the tips of your fingers, where it hurt most.

I remember the coronation of Edward VII in 1910 – at school they put up a tent and we had a real tea party. I stayed at school until I was thirteen; I was very good at writing and arithmetic – that was my thing. My writing was put up on the blackboard for other children to copy and when one of Jim's girls was at the school twenty years after I'd left, she came to me one day and said, 'We've been looking at your writing, Uncle. It's on the blackboard. The teacher said, "We want all you children to write like this."' I said, 'Never!' I was pleased about that.

When I left school in 1911, I started work in a small garden for Mrs Scarlett at Uplands. It's still called Uplands now. I was there one day when Mrs Scarlett's coachman came out into the garden and he said, 'The *Titanic*'s sunk, Fred!' I said, 'Uh? *Titanic*? What's the *Titanic*?' He said, 'It's a boat. It's sunk and they've all gone down with it.' I just got on with the job. Mrs Scarlett used to pay me 4/- a week but when I'd been there two years, she came out and said to me 'I think you'll have to leave, Fred, because you're sixteen and I've got to pay a pension of 2d a week – I can't keep you.'

From there I went to work for Mr Streatfield at the Rocks Estate, where I started as pot boy. I was there when the war started in 1914. I was sixteen and some of my brothers were in the army already. Jim went when he was seventeen. He joined the Royal Garrison Artillery and he was sent out to India, and when he left my sister Emily, who raised us after Mum died, cried all day. He was her favourite, and she didn't want him to leave home. He ended up having eight children in India and he brought them all back home when he retired.

Tom was next to go. He was working at the Rocks Estate. He was a marvellous gardener, Tom was. He went into the East Kents – a Sussex man in the East Kents. He had his arm and leg shattered and he died in France in 1915, and he was buried where he died. One of his comrades buried him on the spot.

Bill joined up the day war broke out. He went to France with the Scots Guards, got frostbitten feet, and they had to cut his boots off. He came home to hospital and he lost two toes but he still had a trigger finger so they sent him back to France. He served right from the beginning of the war up to the last August. He served all those years and then he got killed. It broke my heart when he died – he was the closest to me in age. I think he must have died outright, as we never heard much about wounds or anything like that. Not many years ago they dug him up again and buried him together with Tom. Mum had gone by the time they did that, so she never knew.

I tried to join up when I was only seventeen. I went along to the

Fred Lloyd shortly after joining the Royal Field artillery.

town hall. When I got there, who do you think I should see? My employer at the Rocks Estate – Mr Streatfield! He said, 'What are you doing here, Fred? You should be at work!' He used to call us by our Christian names. He didn't say 'Lloyd' – he called me Fred. He said, 'You shouldn't be here, Fred!' and he took me down a peg or two. I said to him, 'I want to join up – I want to be with my brothers and I want to go to France.' He said, 'You can't go yet – come back next year and I'll see to you.'

So in February 1916, when I was eighteen, I tried to join a Sussex regiment. I was told, 'You can't. You're too short. You're only five foot seven – you have to be five foot eight.' They said I could join the Royal Field Artillery and I said that would do me allright, cos I'd be able to ride horses, even though I'd never touched a horse before.

We did three months training on Salisbury Plain at Stonehenge. The riding master was an old sweat and he just shoved me on the horse and said, 'On you go.' I started off very well but there was a little jump in front of me, and when we got there, he just flicked his hunting crop on the horse's tail and it shot me off. So that was a good start. He made me get back on – you had to be made of tough stuff. The horses were big – good horses. They were hunters mostly – they must have had eight or nine.

It was hard, but I was a fit, strong lad, and used to heavy outdoor work, so I could take it. Most of the other lads came from the slums of London and were in poor shape – ill and undernourished. At the end of the Field Artillery training there was an outbreak of meningitis. It was dreadful. We were all struck down by it and only two of us survived. The rest died or were discharged as unfit for army service because of the shocking after-effects. Many were blind and nearly all of them had lost their hearing – stone deaf for the rest of their lives. I spent months in hospital and was in very poor health for many a year. I'd been A1 fit before, but after I recovered I was classed as C3 – not fit for front-line duty – so I was transferred to the Veterinary Corps. That may have saved my life, because I was deemed unfit for the trenches. Even so, it was no picnic – in fact it was hell on earth.

The Veterinary Corps moved horses to wherever they were needed in France and they wanted help getting them up to the front line – there were no cars at the front line, only horses. So in June 1916, before the Battle of the Somme, twenty of us were taken to Newhaven where we were put on a boat. During the voyage, we were all ordered to get down below. The captain came down and told us why: we were being followed by a German sub. No wonder we were rocking all over the place. Some of the boys started talking about what a lovely meal we'd make for the fish – bloody cheek. But we got there all right – we landed at Le Havre.

From there, we marched off to the Veterinary Corps camp. It was close to the coast, making it handy for getting horses over. There'd been no horses on our boat – it would have stunk! As we marched along, lots of little kids chased us, shouting for coppers. It was marvellous really.

I was detailed with several others to take horses up to the front line, wherever they were needed, and to bring sick horses back. We used to take four at a time: we'd ride one and lead the other three. When we brought the sick horses back, some of them were blind – there were all sorts. It could be a hell of a long way from the front line to the Veterinary Corps in Le Havre – fifty miles sometimes – and it was often pitch dark with lots of obstacles. The sickest horses couldn't go far, so sometimes I'd have to stop on the way, put the horses on a line and get down and try to have a sleep. We were ferrying horses most days and we never got any leave.

The Veterinary Corps was always very kind to their horses – they thought a lot of them. Lots of these horses came from America and Canada. They'd been broken in in England but they arrived rough, smothered in mud and with no shoes. The Veterinary Corps chaps used to shoe them. We used to have to scrub them and that was a hell of a job. Then we'd polish them up and groom them. They had some lovely horses and I often used to scrounge bits of sugar for them. I remember a lot of them coming back in relays from Passchendaele and we used to look after them when they'd come in. Horses understand.

We used horses for almost everything: pulling supplies, food, ammunition, bringing back the dead and wounded and, God knows, there were plenty of them. There was hardly any motor transport, and the animals suffered terribly in that war. I won't say they won the war for us, but we would never have won it without them. When the war started, the government took every horse from all the farms and stables in the land and just left a couple for breeding. From the estate where I worked, they even took a dozen lovely thoroughbred hunters – they only lasted a matter of days on the front line. At one stage so many of them had been killed that we had to bring them in from Canada and South America. The vets had to shoot hundreds of them because they'd gone blind. They put that down to exposure – the bitter cold and non-stop rain. But I dealt with them every day, and I'd swear it was the poison gas that both we and the Germans were using. I've seen horses so broken with fatigue, blind and deafened by the noise of guns that they'd just give up and they'd lie down and die. It was the same as many a soldier on both sides did.

When it was all over, our government sold most of the horses that were left to the French for horsemeat.

I remember reading about the Battle of the Somme in a newspaper that somebody got hold of. I couldn't believe the numbers that got killed – I hadn't joined up for that. I lost friends in the Veterinary Corps – mates used to say, 'Keep your bloody head down!' because we never carried rifles on the horses – we just had to take a chance. At home, I had two shotguns, a 410 and a twelve-bore, and I used to shoot them quite a lot in my job – but not during the war. All I really wanted to do was get back home to my job. All the same, I loved the horses. I still have pictures of them in my room. We lost a few of them and that used to upset me because they were never buried – there was nobody to do the job. It was enough of a job to bury the human beings, never mind the horses. They were just ignored and it used to make me sick. Those beautiful creatures, they didn't deserve to die in those conditions.

On Armistice Day I was in France with my Irish mate and we decided, 'This is a time for a drink.' He was thirty-five and old enough to be my dad. He had five children of his own back in Ireland. That night he got filled up – and locked up. So I lost him. I ended up sleeping on the floor but I had his blanket with me as well as mine, so I was warm enough.

The flu in 1918 was terrible. One of my mates came in one day and said, 'There's a wagon out there, full of French coffins and they're all falling off. Look!' I looked out. They'd taken one of our wagons and filled it to the brim with coffins. We lost one man in the Veterinary Corps – but we didn't know much about him. We just wanted to get home. My Irish mate and I both got the flu. We tramped over a mile in pouring rain to the doctor who was in a little bell tent. We went in one side and came out the other: medicine and duty. We had plenty of duty and no medicine. We walked back in the slush to Le Havre, to our little bits of canvas and I said to my mate, 'I don't know about you, I feel like dying more than anything else. Why don't we find some drink? There's a farm near here – I know the farmer's got some booze. I know cos I've smelt it. I'm going to ask him if he'll sell me a bottle of rum.' Which he did, but he stripped me of all my money. My mate hadn't got any money – he'd spent all of his in a café where he'd gotten drunk and started throwing glasses around. He'd been locked up for that. So we got filled up with rum from the old farmer. My sister had sent me a bottle of Owbridge's Lung Tonic and a chicken. So we had the chicken, the tonic and the rum. And we couldn't get up after that!

After the war was over, they wanted me to stay in the Veterinary Corps. They said I'd done very well. They said, 'We'll put you up for three stripes in the morning and you'll get sergeant's pay straight away, and you could go on to get a commission.' I told them I didn't want a commission and I didn't want any stripes. I wanted to go home to my job. That's all I wanted to do so they let me go, but it was some time before I got home. Still, I got home quicker than most because I had a job to go to. People waited a long time to get home and they were telling lies about who they were going to work for, when they had nobody.

Once I got home after the war, I didn't carry on riding. I went back to my job at the Rocks Estate and I worked up from pot boy to head gardener. I ended up with eight blokes working for me. Mr Streatfield died in 1931 and his wife and daughter both died in 1938 so the place was sold and it became a school run by two old ladies. I stayed with them for many years and when I left, they didn't want me to go. 'You've got a lot of work in you yet, Fred.' 'I know,' I said, 'that's why I want to leave.' So they gave me a hundred quid – which wasn't too bad in those days.

I was forty-one when the second war broke out. They came round and said they were looking for people to join 'Dad's Army', so I joined the Home Guard and became an air raid warden in Uckfield. There were no bombs on Uckfield but I saw one German plane shot down. It was very hard work because I still had my own job to do during the day. One night, the air raid siren went twelve times and I had to get on me bike every time to get up to my warden's post.

I have one son and I remember how worried I was about him during the Second World War. When he joined up, he went to Blackpool to train and he said he wanted to be an air gunner. He went right through his air gunner training but he was so good at Morse code that they decided to train him as a wireless operator. One day he came home and he was crying because he still wanted to be an air gunner. I said, 'You don't want to be a bloody air gunner! You stay as a wireless operator! Stay on the ground!' So that's what he did.

After that war was over, I carried on as head gardener on the Rocks Estate and I had seven Land Army girls piled onto me to work in the garden and clean the place up. I had four men working there as well but the girls were not really interested in gardening. I had to get rid of them because they were fiddling my books for the time they were putting in, and I didn't like that. It wasn't fair on the men.

Alice, my wife, died in 1989. We were married for sixty-eight years. We met when her dad moved to Uckfield and took a job at the Rocks Estate as house carpenter. She had two sisters and a brother, George, who was killed in the First World War. When my son was born in 1922, I named him Frederick George, after my wife's brother, and William, after my brother. He comes to see me every three weeks and he's been a very good son. From him I've got six great-great-grandchildren. He's got two hip replacements and he'll be eighty-three in March 2005.

I smoked from the time I was sixteen until I was a hundred and four. That's when I gave up. At sixteen, I started smoking cigarettes but when I married Dorothy at twenty-one – she was twenty-two – I said, 'I'm going to smoke a pipe.' And she said, 'That's right, you smoke a pipe – I like pipe smoke.' I used to smoke Gizzard's. It was five pence an ounce. So I smoked for ninety years – I smoked all the time – and it never killed me. But I gave it up a year ago and I haven't smoked since. In fact, my neighbour came to see me recently and said, 'I know a man who's nearly ninety who wants to *start* smoking.' I wanted to help. I said, 'I've got the very thing for him. I've got a pipe I bought for £10, I've got half an ounce of tobacco, I've got loads of pipe cleaners, a box of matches; I've got everything and it's all here in this bag. You give this to the old man!' When my neighbour last came round she said, 'He smokes now and he enjoys it!'

I've got a terrific appetite these days. I clear my plate every day – I don't send anything back – I remember what we had to eat during the war. For breakfast – bully beef. Lunch was bully beef and bully beef for dinner. It came in these big tins and in hot weather you'd be able to pour it out. They gave us bread sometimes and they gave us cheese but I never ate it. I always used to swap it. That's because when I was very small, my brother Jack said, 'That's sour milk, Fred.' I always remembered that and said to myself, 'I'm not eating sour milk.' So I've never touched it. Jack was nine years older than me. He was wounded by a piece of shrapnel in the war but he died when he was ninety-three. So you don't need cheese to live a long life.

I've had a very lucky life. I've enjoyed it – and I'm still enjoying it. In the last few years lots of people have come to talk to me. I like them to come. It's marvellous. But then I like talking.

Even after all the horrors of the war I've retained my faith. Do I believe in God? Yes, I do. Perhaps he's not 'real' but I like to think he's there. I prayed during the war – I prayed when I was going to France on that boat and we were being followed by the submarine. And in France, I prayed when I was frightened. I used to get very frightened – I expect I shouldn't have done and I should have been braver. Sometimes I felt a bit of a coward but I did my best. I did what I was asked and I was praised for it.

I often think about my brother William – Bill. He used to hold my hand when we went to school . . . It broke my heart when he died. I would have liked to have died with him – but I didn't, and here I am today.

Harry Patch

Duke of Cornwall's Light Infantry · *Born* 17 June 1898

I was born in Bath on 17 June 1898. I had two brothers and no sisters. The oldest one was ten years older than me, and the middle one was five years older than me. He was a regular soldier in the Royal Engineers and was wounded at Mons and didn't go back again. He told me what the trenches were like, and I didn't want to go. My oldest brother had asthma so he didn't pass the medical, but he was on munitions. He died a few years ago, aged ninety-six. My mother was one of a family of six and all of them lived to be over ninety. My other brother died at about eighty-four.

I went to Coombe Down School. It was a Church of England school. When I first went to school, we had a headmaster with a long white beard who seemed about 150 years old and eventually the time came when he retired. He was replaced by a fellow from just outside Trowbridge: Bertie Collins. He was a disciplinarian – so much so that he lost two teachers in three months. They couldn't stick it. But I met him, oh, forty years later and he was a good man.

He gave up two nights a week, Tuesday and Thursday, for evening classes. His one condition was that if you started, you had to stick it. First hour on the Tuesday was English as it is spoken. The second hour was Latin. Anyway, we stuck it, and Thursday first hour was geometry, and the second hour was algebra. He asked us the shortest distance between two points, A and B, and of course the answer was a straight line. He told us to write down the definition of a curve. Well I couldn't think so I wrote, 'straight line with a bend in it', and he gave me a rap across the knuckles. Some years later, I was at a house just outside Yeovil, at Brimton D'Arcy, and over the door was a stone with a motto carved in Latin. I was talking to the owner of the house and he said, 'I wish I knew what that Latin meant.' 'You don't know, sir?' I asked. 'No,' he said so I told him that it meant 'Not eloquently great, but vivacious or cheerful.' He looked at me. 'Where did you learn that? You ought to have been a Latin teacher.'

We used to walk to school. It was no distance. I was fifteen when I left, but I continued to study afterwards. At eighteen I sat for the registered plumber's certificate, passed it, and after the war I carried on studying and I got the MRSI – which was Member of the Royal Sanitary Institute. That meant I had the qualifications to work as a sanitary engineer.

When the war broke out I was sixteen, and at eighteen I was called up. I had six months training at Sutton Vealy, just outside Warminster, with the 33rd Training Battalion. On the rifle range, I needed eight points to be a marksman. I may not have been interested in being a marksman, but I was interested in the 6d a day extra. Anyway, I needed eight marks, and I said to the sergeant, 'This rifle is firing high, can I lower the sights?' We were on the 600 mark range. He said, 'I don't know – I'll ask the officer.' So he came and he said, 'Lower them to 550.' I did and my next two shots were bull's eyes. That gave me twelve points – four more than I needed so I didn't trouble a damn where my next shots went – I think I missed the target. Anyway, when I got to France, I was put on the Lewis Gun.

I'll always remember morning inspection in the trenches. That was very severe. They used to come round and your gun had to be clean, well oiled and loaded. Ready for immediate action. The inspecting officer would take the revolver out and snap it open. If there were six rounds left, OK. But if one was gone, he'd say, 'Who ordered you to fire that? What did you fire at? Did you hit it?' If you had six rounds, you were allright. If you had one gone, you had to account for it, because if you had an NCO or an officer that you didn't like, one round was all it took. It never happened to us, as far as I know . . .

On my nineteenth birthday, 17 June 1917, we were in the trenches at Passchendaele. We didn't go into action, but I saw it all happen. Haig put a three-day barrage on the Germans, and thought, 'Well, there can't be much left of them.' I think it was the Yorkshires and Lancashires that went over. I watched them as they came out of their dugouts and the German machine guns just mowed them down. I doubt whether any of them reached the front line.

A couple of weeks after that we moved to Pilckem Ridge. I can still see the bewilderment and fear on the men's faces as we went over the top. We crawled because if you stood up you'd be killed. All over the battlefield the wounded were lying there, English and German, all crying for help. But we weren't like the Good Samaritan in the Bible, we were the robbers who passed by and left them. You couldn't stop to help them. I came across a Cornishman who was ripped from shoulder to his waist with shrapnel, his stomach on the ground beside him. A bullet wound is clean – shrapnel tears you all to pieces. As I got to him he said, 'Shoot me.' Before I could draw my revolver, he died. I was with him for the last sixty seconds of his life. He gasped one word – 'Mother'. That one word has run through my brain for eighty-eight years. I will never forget it. I think it is the most sacred word in the English language. It wasn't a cry of distress or pain – it was one of surprise and joy. I learned later that his mother was already dead, so he felt he was going to join her.

We got as far as their second line and four Germans stood up. They didn't get up to run away, they got up to fight. One of them came running towards me. He couldn't have had any ammunition or he would have shot me, but he came towards me with his bayonet pointing at my chest. I fired and hit him in the shoulder. He dropped his rifle, but still came stumbling on. I can only suppose that he wanted to kick our Lewis Gun into the mud, which would have made it useless. I had three live rounds left in my revolver and could have killed him with the first. What should I do? I had seconds to make my mind up. I gave him his life. I didn't kill him. I shot him above the ankle and above the knee and brought him down. I knew he would be picked up, passed back to a POW camp, and at the end of the war he would rejoin his family. Six weeks later, a countryman of his killed my three mates. If that had happened before I met that German, I would have damn well killed him. But we never fired to kill. My Number One, Bob, used to keep the gun low and wound them in the legs – bring them down. Never fired to kill them. As far as I know he never killed a German. I never did either. Always kept it low.

We were soon back in the trenches after that action. Our living conditions there were lousy, dirty and unsanitary – no matter what the weather was, whether it was hot or cold, rain or fine, you were in there for four days, and three nights. There were rats as big as cats, and if you had any leather equipment the damn things would gnaw at it. We had leather equipment – and they'd chew it. If you stood still long enough they'd chew your bootlaces.

Lice. We were lousy. The lice were the size of grains of rice, each with its own bite, each with its own itch. When we could, we would run hot wax from a candle down the seams of our trousers, our vests – whatever you had – to burn the buggers out. It was the only thing to do. Eventually, when we got to Rouen, coming back, they took every stitch off us and gave us a suit of sterilised blue material. And the uniforms they took off, they burned them – to get rid of the lice. For the four months I was in France I never had a bath, and I never had any clean clothes to put on. Nothing.

Our rations – you were lucky if you got some bully beef and a biscuit. You couldn't get your teeth into it. Sometimes if they shelled the supply lines you didn't get anything for days on end. There were five in a machine-gun team, and everything we had was shared amongst us. I used to get a parcel from home. My mother knew the grocer pretty well. There was always an ounce of tobacco and two packets of twenty cigarettes. That was handed to Number One to share out. That ounce of tobacco – Number Three was a pipe-smoker, same as I was – was cut in half. He had half and I had half. The cigarettes – thirteen each for the others and they took it in turns to have the odd one. And if you got a pair of socks, and somebody else had a pair with holes in, they'd chuck them away and they'd have the new ones. That was the life we lived because we never knew from one moment to the next when something would come over with our number on.

You talked to your mates in the team. There was always a certain amount of chatter. Nerves, you might call it. I used to think, shall we get through tomorrow, or shall we get a packet? Am I going up the line tonight, will I be coming back? It's dark and everything may be quiet now, but am I going to see the sun come up in the morning? And when the sun comes up in the morning, shall I see it set at night? At some point you showed your emotions. That was why our comradeship was so important, because I was scared more or less all the time I was out there.

We were part of the battalion, but at the same time we were a little crowd on our own. You could talk to your pals about anything and everything. I mean, these boys were with you night and day, you shared everything with them. We each knew where the others came from, what their lives had been and where they were. You were one of them – we belonged to each other. It's a difficult thing to describe, the comradeship between us. I never met any of their people or any of their parents, but I knew all about them, and they knew all about me and mine. There was nothing that cropped up, doesn't matter what it was, that you couldn't discuss with them in one way or another. If you scrounged anything, you always shared it with them. You could confide everything to them. They would understand. Letters from home, when we got them, if there was any trouble in them, they would discuss it with you.

Drink was either weak tea or water drunk from old petrol cans. As for food, we had Crosse & Blackwell's plum and apple jam and dog biscuits. The biscuits were so hard we used to throw them away. One day I looked through the metal aperture that we used to fire through, and two dogs were out there fighting over one of our biscuits. They were fighting over which one should have it. Their owners had probably been killed by shell fire. They were simply strays. They were fighting over a biscuit to keep alive. I thought to myself, 'Well, I don't know, there's two animals out there fighting for their lives, and here we are, two highly civilised nations, and what are we fighting over?'

We were there to do our job. We were Lewis gunners. I was Number Two. Our Number One, Bob, who fired the gun, was looking for a Number Two. His Number Two had gone home on compassionate leave, and the sergeant in charge of us said, 'Here's somebody has some training on the Lewis Gun. Here's a Number Two for you.' I was to be in charge of the ammunition and the working parts of the gun. Bob told me, 'You've got to do the job thoroughly and correctly. Our lives depend on it.' We'd do alternate turns of four nights and three days in the trenches, then four days behind the lines to rest and recuperate.

On 21 September, the night I was wounded, the battalion had been relieved at ten o'clock and we were going back over open ground to the support line. The shell that got us was what we called a whizz-bang, which burst amongst us. The force of it threw me to the floor, but I didn't realise I'd been hit for a few minutes. The burning hot metal knocks the pain out of you at first but I soon saw blood, so I put a field dressing on it. Then the pain started.

I didn't know what had happened to the others at first, but I was told later that I had lost three of my mates. That shell killed Numbers Three, Four and Five. We were a little team together, and those men who were carrying the ammunition were blown to pieces. I reacted very badly. It was like losing a part of my life. It upset me more than anything. We had only been together four months, but with hell going on around us, it seemed like a lifetime.

I'd got this piece of shrapnel right in the groin. It was about two inches long, half an inch thick, with a jagged edge. I was taken to a dressing station and I lay there all that night and the next day, until the evening. The wound had been cleaned and they had smeared it with something to keep the lice away. When the doctor came to see me, he could actually see the shrapnel. 'Would you like me to take that out of your leg?' he asked, but added quickly, 'Before you answer "Yes", there's no anaesthetic in the camp. None whatever. It's been used on people more badly wounded than you are. Yours is only a scratch.' So I thought for a minute or two, and said, 'How long will you be?' He said, 'A couple of minutes.' So I said, 'Carry on.' Four fellows grabbed me – one on each arm and one on each leg – and I can feel that bloody knife even now, cutting out that shrapnel. When he pulled it out, the doctor asked me if I wanted to keep the shrapnel as a souvenir. Officer or not, I swore at him, 'I've had the bloody thing too long already. Throw it away!'

The fellow in the next bed to me said, 'If he writes anything in that book on the table, you're for Blighty.' The word Blighty meant everything to us soldiers. I didn't believe him, but he wrote something in the green book, and some hours later somebody came in, called my name and number and I was sent to Rouen, where they put us in a warehouse. You could see the hospital ship from there, but it didn't sail that night. There were rumours of a submarine in the Channel, so we sailed the next day and came in to Southampton. Because of my wound I never returned to France.

We arrived in Southampton on a foggy morning. We were met by the Salvation Army. They were doing a good job. They gave us blankets and cups of tea. The women were coming round with post-cards already written that we could send home. You had a choice of postcard – 'wounded seriously' or 'wounded slightly'. The Red Cross came along, asking, 'Where is your nearest military hospital?' Well, my home was Bath, and the main hospital in Bath was a military hospital. So I said, 'Bath,' and thought, 'This is it – I'm going home.' I was half unconscious and half asleep, but I thought, 'This train is a long time getting from Southampton to Bath.' Eventually they unloaded us. I said to the orderly, 'Where are we?' He said, 'This is Lime Street, Liverpool.' That was as near as I got to Bath.

I was in hospital until Christmas and then I had a leave and went to Bodmin. I was there a few weeks and then I was transferred back to Sutton Coldfield, Birmingham. There I met two fellows from Bath in the Somerset Light Infantry: Titch Harding and Bill Taylor. Bill's people had a building business in Olfield Park. We started in Green Section, and then went to Yellow, and then Red. When you got to Red, then you were fit. Anyway, we were in the Yellow Section. They told us we'd got seven days' leave. I think they were glad to get rid of us. So the three of us decided to go to Bath together.

We got to the train station and we gave Titch our railway warrants. 'You get the tickets. Bill and I will find a coach.' Well, we found a coach for just us three travelling. We got down as far as Hereford and you could hear the guard coming down, slamming the doors and examining the tickets. Titch put his hand in his pocket and pulled out two tickets. He couldn't find the other one. He said it must have gone through a hole in his pocket. 'We'll find it before we get to Bristol.' He struck a match, blew it out and broke it in half. He took two other matches, broke them in half and put all of them in his hat. He shook them up and said, 'Whoever draws the spent match has to hide from the guard under the seat. The other two will hide his kitbag.' So anyway Bill drew the spent match. He went under the seat and we put our kitbags down. The guard came along. Titch put his hand in his pocket, pulled out the tickets and gave them to the guard. He pulled out three tickets. The other one had reappeared. 'Three of you?' said the guard. 'Where's your mate? Gone along the corridor or something?' 'No,' said Titch, 'he's a bit rocky upstairs. You go and shut the door quietly and he'll be allright.' 'Where is he?' asked the guard. 'He's under the seat,' said Titch.

You've heard of *Murder on the Orient Express*? Well there was damn near murder on the Great Western Railway when Bill came out from under the seat. I knew those men until they died, back at Bath in civil life, and Bill never lived that down. We cooled him down a bit on the way to Bristol but when we got there, the guard stirred things up again. He called a redcap over and said, 'You see these three on the train for Bath? One of them's a bit rocky upstairs.' So we were led to a sergeant who was standing on the platform. 'Hello, what's the matter with these three? Travelling without a pass?' said the sergeant. 'No,' said the redcap, 'passes are allright, but one of them's a bit rocky.' 'Get back on duty,' said the sergeant, 'and I'll take them over.' So he took charge of us. At Bath we were met by our people. A week later, at the end of our leave, we got off the train at Bristol where we were met by the same sergeant. 'Hello, you three,' he said. 'Enjoy your leave?' 'Yeah,' we said. 'Good. Now come along with me,' and the sergeant carried Bill's kitbag. He took us over to the train, told the guard to take care of us, told the driver about his special passengers and before long the driver had told the Orderly Room and the Orderly Room spread it all round our camp and soon everyone heard that Bill was 'a bit rocky'.

'A bit rocky' was an expression you heard, but nobody ever used the phrase 'shell shock'. Somebody was wounded – but never 'shell-shocked'.

After that I stayed at the camp. I went through Red, which meant I was fit, and I was taken on route marches. No sooner had I got on the full equipment, I had a pain up the side. I went sick and the doctor gave me seven days' excused duty. During those seven days there was a parade I didn't attend and the sergeant major put me on the crime sheet. Nobody liked this sergeant major. None of us, not even the officers.

Instead of going in front of the officer, I went sick again. I saw the doctor, who said, 'I thought I gave you seven days' leave yesterday?' 'You did, sir.' 'Then what the devil are you doing here again?' So I told him. 'Who put you on a crime sheet?' he asked. 'Sergeant Major Smithers, sir.' 'Oh,' he said, 'you tell the sergeant major what he can do with his crime sheet,' and he gave me explicit instructions as to where he should stick it. So I went in front of the company commander, who told me that he'd had a word with the doctor and he dismissed the case against me. 'Did the doctor say anything else to you?' he asked. 'No, sir,' I said. 'You're sure?' I thought for a moment and said, 'Well, he did give me a message for the sergeant major, but I don't care to repeat it. There's ladies in the room.' 'If he gave you a message for the sergeant major,' said the company commander, 'you will repeat it – and that is an order!' I had to repeat it or I'd have ended up back on the crime sheet. So he called in the sergeant major and I told him exactly what the doctor said. Well that didn't go down at all well. So it was 'Left turn, quick march'– and I was out. Any dirty job after that, I was, on it. That went all round the camp. It was, 'What about Patch then, he told the sergeant major where he could stuff his crime sheet.'

While I was in Birmingham, they sent me to a hospital just outside the city. I always said my first wife was an 'army pick-up'. What happened was, Titch and I were running for a bus to get back to Sutton Coldfield at the same time as these two girls were coming down the steps from a cinema. I ran into one and knocked her down. I picked her up and we started talking. Her name was Ada Billington, but she told me to call her Bobby. It was a dry evening, and she was going on the same bus that we were. We met up again the next night and went for a walk. The night after that I was supposed to meet her again but that was the day I was sent to the hospital. When I got to the hospital, I said to the nurse, 'Would you ring this number and tell them that I can't meet Bobby tonight? Say I'm in hospital.' At half past five that afternoon, Bobby came to visit me. She was on night duty. She carried on coming to see me every night after that. The nurse spotted it. She said, 'The girl who comes to see you, is she a relation?' I said 'No' and I told her how I met her. 'Oh,' she said, 'we've had a lot of them in here. Usually they visit a couple of times, then they find somebody in khaki to take them out. You're the first two real lovers we've had.' She told the ward sister. The ward sister told the matron, and so it went on. When I was sent to the Isle of Wight, they came to see me off, and said, 'You know our address. We know your girl's address.' I told them that we'd keep in touch. They said that if they were still in England after the war and we still wanted to get married, they would attend our wedding. When we did get married, they came to our wedding. We got married on 13 September 1918. I'd known Bobby for about a year by then. We were married for the next fifty-seven years, and we had two children.

After Birmingham, I was sent to Bareham Downs near Tadworth. I finished my training there, and after that I went to Gordonhill Fort on the Isle of Wight. I was on draft to go back a second time, when the Armistice was signed. We were on the range, and the range was at some distance from the fort, and they said at the fort, 'If the Armistice is signed, we'll send a rocket up.' We were watching and, sure enough, we saw the rocket. We had some spare ammunition with us and the sergeant said, 'Well, we don't want to carry it back. Fire it. Fire it out over the sea. You won't do any damage.' The fellow next to me started firing off his rifle. I asked him what he was firing at. 'That hut at the end of the range,' he said. 'You damn fool!' I shouted. 'The markers are in there!' They were lying on the floor of the hut and he was pumping live ammunition at them. When that Armistice was signed, I don't know whether I was pleased or just relieved that it I didn't have to go back to those lousy trenches.

When I joined up, they had me in uniform, square-bashing within three days. Coming out of the army was very different. It took me five months to leave. While we were on the Isle of Wight, the order came through that nobody who had seen active service would go back to France a second time. C Company of the battalion, made up of people coming out of hospital, got to be one hundred strong. One day, our officer got us out and ordered us to double round the square. Nobody liked this officer and half the company were at the double but the other half only marched. The officer didn't know what the hell to do. We got back to camp and decided, 'We're not going on parade again. We joined the army for the duration of the war. Now the war is over. We're not going on.' The sergeant major came down the line of huts and shouted, 'On parade, C Company.' Somebody threw a boot at him and he was wise enough not to come back. But the officer came back, pulled his revolver out and said, 'The first man who refuses to go on parade, I'll shoot him.' Nobody said anything.

No one moved and we stayed in our huts. That afternoon we were on the range, so we divided up the ammunition. I went back and asked for the officer again. He came out and raised his revolver. I heard a click on the trigger, but at that moment, bang – thirty bolts went back. Somebody in the crowd shouted, 'Now shoot, you bugger, if you dare.' We were had up for mutiny. We had an officer come over from the mainland. I think he was a brigadier or a general or something. He listened to the officer. 'I've heard the officer's side of it,' he said, 'now I'd like to listen to the men.' So he picked out thirty men who went behind a screen so they shouldn't be recognised, and the men told him what they thought. After that, C Company ended up doing nothing but parades around the camp.

We were then sent to Gosport. We got there late at night but there were no blankets for us, so we started to kick up a row. Somebody asked, 'Where are you from?' And somebody replied, 'Duke of Cornwall's, Gordonhill Fort, and we'll kick up a bloody row here if we don't get a blanket.' They issued us all with three white blankets, without government marks on them. Everybody in Gosport next day had a blanket. We went from there to Havant, and that's where we got our papers.

After the war I took the exam to be a sanitary engineer. I worked for Longs until 1939. By then, I was forty-one and too old for the Second World War. I saw an advert looking for a sanitary engineer. The colonel-in-chief of the housing camp at Yeovil wanted someone over military age who had the necessary qualifications. I had the qualifications, so I took the job and that's what brought me down here to just outside Street. I bought a partnership and became sanitary engineer in all the camps such as Street and Glastonbury. Some were billets, some were camps. They were all full of Americans for the six months before D-Day. I had to sign the Official Secrets Act, because I knew the movement of every troop. I knew when they left here, where they went and who was coming in. I knew all the movements except one – D-Day itself. I didn't know anything about that. We left the camp one night and everything was normal. We came back the next day and there was not a troop to be seen. The range in the kitchen was still on, the fires were still going, urns of tea, coffee and cocoa were still hot. There was sugar, butter, cheese. We didn't know what to do with it all. In the end we gave a lot of it to the local people. We were left with a lot of American stuff – three-foot levels, forks, spades, all sorts of things. We sent them to a company in Taunton and they returned it all back to us. 'We don't want this; this is American.' So in the end, to tell you the truth, we bloody sold it. Those Americans never came back, of course.

I worked until I was sixty-five. When I retired, we had ten plumbers and eighteen hot-water fitters working for us. We used to do a lot of work for Somerset County Council. Schools and that. What I said was law! The senior partner said to me, 'You've got your health and strength, Harry, why don't you carry on?' I told him, 'I've got my health and strength, and that's the time to enjoy life. I've had fifty years in the building trade and that's enough.' After I retired, we had a hell of a big garden. Too big. I lived a short distance from the senior partner. He had a small garden and he and his wife and daughter used to come to my garden and work in it. Give him a pair of secateurs and he was happy.

My wife died in 1976. After she died, my oldest son turned alcoholic on whisky. He'd done twenty-two years in the navy. He came out and got a job with Clarks, the shoe people. He took early redundancy there. He had a naval pension, a pension from Clarks plus

Harry Patch, 107 at the time of publication, remains
a committed ambassador for conciliation and loses
no opportunity to underline the futility of war and the
tragedy of the loss of young lives.

redundancy pay. A friend from the British Legion said to me, 'There's only one problem with your Denis – he's got too much money.' He never married, and my home was his home. And of course when my wife died, and without a will, everything came to me. Denis wasn't violent, but nothing was right for him. Even though we had a very good home helper who cleaned our bungalow from A to Z, he'd get the vacuum cleaner out when he got home and clean it all again. Eventually he sold everything that he could in that bungalow – silver and all – to get whisky, and in the end he came to me. I'd married a second time by then and he came to me and my wife, and said, 'Look at my legs.' My wife looked at his legs, and said, 'You ought to see the doctor with those.' 'I'll make an appointment tomorrow,' said Denis. 'You'll do no such thing,' said my wife, 'you'll pick up that telephone on the table and you'll make an appointment for the doctor to come and see you.' So the doctor came. Denis had a pal – a boozing pal, who used to drive me around sometimes. The pal said to me, 'I think you ought to know, Mr Patch, I was in the room when the doctor saw Denis. He's got cirrhosis of the liver and we'll have to get him to London as soon as we can. I can't discuss his case, I'm not his doctor. You ring Doctor Stevens and he'll tell you.' So I rang the doctor. He said, 'Yes, we'll get him to London as soon as we can – but I'm afraid it's too late.' 'Too late for what?' I asked. 'He's got a fortnight to live,' said the doctor. Denis lived for another eight days. He was forty-five.

I married my second wife when I was eighty-one. She died three years ago. The lady with me is my friend now. She's lovely – she's ninety. A good companion for me. She's from London.

When I first came to the home where I'm living today, the room I had was right opposite a linen cupboard, and if I was half asleep, half awake, directly they switched that light on, it flickered, and it reminded me of the flash of a bomb. I've got over it now. It just takes some time.

Even eighty-eight years afterwards I still remember. I still commemorate 21 September and remember the three friends I lost. They are always with me. I don't do anything. I don't feel like talking. I've always remembered it. I don't join in when people sing all the old songs and I don't watch war films. Why should I? I was there. I can see that damned explosion now.

With Passchendaele, the sights I saw on that battlefield and again at Pilckem – I lost all faith in the Church of England. But that boy's cry, 'Mother', brought it all back. I realised then, and I realise now, death is not the end. Death is like a one-way street you go down, but don't come back. Death is not the end.

I always swore I would never return to the scene of the battle but then I was invited to go to the 75th anniversary of the opening of the Menin Gate. Do you know that was the first time in my life I got a passport? The first time I went to Belgium, a rifle was all I needed. In the countryside you could see just where the trenches were. It had all been filled in but we found the spot, near enough where I was wounded. It was a potato patch. It was a sobering moment, reading all those names on the Menin Gate. But the sad thing was that so few of us knew each others' surnames. We used first names and nicknames. I couldn't find my old mates. But I see their faces in my dreams.

Last year I went back to Ypres, where I met one of the last surviving German veterans of the war, Charles Kuentz, who was 107. It was very emotional. We had both been on the same battlefield at Pilckem Ridge. For a while I hadn't wanted to meet him, but I got a letter from him in Germany and he seemed like a nice man and I decided I would meet him. He *was* a nice man and we talked, then we both sat in silence, staring out at the landscape. Both of us remembering the stench, the noise, the gas, the mud crusted with blood, the cries of the fallen comrades. We had both fought because we were told to. Sadly he died a year after I met him.

Why should the British government call me up and take me out to a battlefield to shoot a man I never knew, whose language I couldn't speak? All those lives lost for a war finished over a table. Now what is the sense in that? It's just an argument between two governments. Neither Charles nor I ever want any other young man ever to go through what we did again, but still we send our lads to war. In Iraq, our young men are being killed and told to kill.

I don't think it is possible to truly explain the bond that is forged between a soldier in the trenches and his fellow soldiers. There you all are, no matter what your life in civvy street, covered in lice, desperately hungry, eking out the small treats – the ounce of tobacco, the biscuit. You relied on him and he on you, never really thinking that it was just the same for the enemy. But it was. It was every bit as bad.

William Roberts

Royal Flying Corps · *Born* 29 September 1900, *died* 30 April 2006

I was born in Hartlepool, County Durham. I had a brother and a sister. My sister, Florence, lived to seventy but my brother died when he was very young. I remember playing under a table with him. We put a cover across and played tents. We really enjoyed that. When he died, a horse and cab came and took him away. I remember him being carried into the cab through a door at the side. I wasn't supposed to see it – I was very young. They buried him on the edge of the old town.

I started school in 1903. I remember my first day. I can see myself now. It was a beautiful sunny morning and we didn't live very far away. I can remember walking there with my mother. I was in my shorts. When I got there, the teacher gave me some shells to play with. I remember a boy called Maley who I didn't like at all. He was horrible.

When I left school, I worked for the *Northern Daily Mail* as a copy-taker. I used to make five shillings and sixpence a week. My job was to read copy with an old man, and correct it. In the morning, I would get to work before him and get the little stove going. That's where I was when Hartlepool was bombarded by German warships on 16 December 1914. We were sitting at the table in this big room with loads of windows. A chap called Freddie, a lino-typist, came in and suddenly there was a BOOOOM, and Freddie looked at me and said, 'Scarper, young un.' Well, I got my overcoat, because it was very cold, and I had to run ziggy-zag through the streets to get home. As I ran, shrapnel pinged against a Fry's Chocolate sign next to me. I passed a woman who had run out into the street, stark naked. I had never ever seen a naked woman before. Then another woman came out of her house and sat on the kerb with her baby in her arms. I ran past the school which had a large hole in the wall made by a shell that had entered, but didn't explode. Eventually, I got home.

As the bombardment started, my cousin Alf's family ran from their house, to get away from the sea front and away from the guns. Alf's younger brother was hit by a shell which shattered his arm. One of his pals had his right foot shattered. Alf ripped his brother's shirt off, put a tourniquet on this arm and carried him to the hospital. It's funny because when I think back to my childhood, I can remember how German bands used to come to Hartlepool in the summertime and play in those very same streets.

Alf later became the headmaster of the school that we attended as children. He was a funny man. He used to sleep with his eyes open.

My dad was in the Royal Engineers. He joined in August 1914. I remember his number was 43968. One day in 1915 I went with my mother, who originally came from the Dudley area, to stay with her relations in Birmingham. While we were there, we got news that my dad was home at a barracks just outside London, and we could see him there. He had his week's leave with us – and then it was 'Cheerio' – and that was it. I never saw him again. He was due home from the trenches in December 1915, but he never came. A German sniper got him.

After that, I wanted to join up. I wanted to join the Durham Light Infantry, but they wouldn't entertain having me. I was too young, sixteen, I think. Eventually, when I was seventeen, I joined the Royal Flying Corps. I thought I was a big man but I got a shock. I was sent to Laffans Plain at Farnborough, where they had no accommodation indoors so we were all under canvas, near the aircraft repair factory. My job was to maintain the aircraft engines. My number was 81853. Not bad for my age, to remember that, eh?

They used to take the planes out, fly them and test them. Rather than go to the bother of putting ballast in, they'd take a passenger up with them: usually one of us youngsters who wanted to fly. One beautiful sunny day, it was my turn. The aerodrome was a blaze of blue sky and green grass. We were in an old Maurice Farman pusher machine with the engine at the back. A great big thing – I'd never been in one before. I listened to the engine and we started to move. I looked up at the beautiful blue sky, when suddenly, there was this loud ZOOM and I was hanging upside down, staring at the ground. I undid my safety belt and fell flat on my head. The plane had gone completely over. The pilot was a Belgian officer. He got me by the shoulder and he said, 'Run away, because it'll go up in flames – and if the fuel goes over you, it's worse.' And I did run. An hour later, that same pilot took up another plane, which crashed and killed him.

I must have seen five planes crash around the aerodrome. None

William Roberts, whose father's death by a sniper's bullet inspired him to join up, aged just 16.

of this deterred me though. I went up again and again. I once looped
the loop in a BE2c. As a mechanic, I used to work on Avros, Bristol
Scouts, BE2c's and Sopwith Camels with the rotary engines – all
sorts of aircraft.

At Farnborough we used to go into the work shops, and then
we'd come out of the flight sheds and do a bit of drill. But we didn't
want to march and we used to skive off into the huts and play shove
halfpenny. The army huts had a door at each end so when the officers
came round and opened a door at one end, we would scarper out
the door at the other end. There was one time when a Manchester lad
and I tried to run out of the near door but we were caught by the
corporal who was escorting the officer. We had to fall in. I was given
one hundred and sixty-eight hours detention in the digger for that.
I couldn't refuse. I'd have been shot.

When you were caught, they didn't trust you to give your name
so they grabbed your cap and took your number. They didn't think
you might be wearing someone else's cap! The hut where I was
imprisoned was covered with sheets of metal – just like a steel cage
– and it had little windows. When teatime came, I heard a bit of a
tinkling noise, and I had a look up and there was a piece of string
hanging down with a couple of Woodbines tied on. It was from some
of the girls from the office.

At mealtimes, the order came: 'To your doors'. The doors were all
open and we took a step forward and it was left and right turn. Then
you'd walk round past the table and you'd pick your dinner up.
You'd get your potatoes and the veg, and you waited until you had
the order to take a step back and then you ate your dinner. The
latrines were a sheet of metal with a door at the back. If you opened
the door, you could see a certain part of a person. I had trouble from

one of the corporals while I was in there. He was such a nasty type that I ended up pinning him against the door.

I was in the digger for about a week. I spent most of my time burning stuff – incinerating. The unbelievable thing is that I was released after a week and I was just changing into my working tackle to get back to the workshops, when the corporal came over and said, 'Roberts, you're wanted in the orderly room.' 'What have I done wrong now?' I asked. So I went back to the officer in the orderly room, and the officer said a few words, and he made me a corporal! Two stripes on my overcoat. Unbelievable. I was a corporal!

When the Royal Air Force was formed in 1918, made up of the Royal Flying Corps and the Royal Naval Air Service, we in the Royal Flying Corps were the commoners. The Royal Naval Air Service didn't like us. They used to wear collars and ties. We wore tunics.

At one point, discipline had become slack and they wanted NCOs to volunteer as drill instructors or physical training instructors. I was quite a clever fencer – in fact I used to fence with Sergeant Major Storey, who was the fencing champion at the Olympics. So I went to Cranwell to train as a gym instructor. I passed out first class. As an instructor, I used to take the girls. I'm not sure about women soldiers; I don't think they like to dirty their hands. All the same, when I used to say 'left leg raised', they used to like that and giggle.

Not long before I was discharged, I was sent for tests and examinations as a pilot. I was sent to Harley Street in London. I remember an orderly escorting me and leaving me standing outside a room. The door opened, all darkness, and a voice said, 'Whatever you hear, reply.' I heard the door close and a voice said, 'God Save the King.' After that, they put me in a chair and strapped me up to stop me falling. On the other side of the room there was a shelf, carrying a big weight. It was ever so quiet and the weight moved suddenly and it came across at me. I didn't admit it, but that really frightened me. After that, the doctor came along with a little mallet and hit me on the knee – bang, bang, bang.

A few days later, I was told by an officer that I had passed all my tests and that I was to begin training at the flying school on the following Monday. I said 'No.' I'd passed all the tests but I didn't want it. I wanted civvy street, so I came out of the service.

Before I'd joined the Royal Flying Corps and after I'd worked at the newspaper, I'd been an indentured apprentice marine engineer. When I joined the Royal Flying Corps, I broke my apprenticeship. After the war, there was a scheme called the broken apprenticeship scheme and I was able to continue. So I worked on ships' engines but as soon as I'd got through and got my indentures, that's it; I was sacked. There was no work. It was a bad show. So what did I do? I went back to the air force.

I went back into the air force on the motor transport side. I realised in civvy street that that was where the money was. I got my former rank. They called me leading aircraftsman which was equivalent to a corporal during the war. I met Lawrence of Arabia at this time. He was quiet, very quiet – an unassuming person. If you met him, you'd think he was nobody.

After I came out of the air force a second time, the real business was motor cars. I made a beeline for a garage. I had a motorbike and I went up to Halifax where my people had moved. One evening we were in a pub, having a few drinks, and I picked up a newspaper and looked at the vacancies. A motor mechanic was wanted at a place called Sorby Bridge, which I didn't know. So next morning I showed up at seven o'clock, waiting for the manager to open up. He had a chat with me and I started right away. I had no overalls, but I jumped on my motorbike and went to see my sister's husband who let me have some. My first job was to take a Maudsley lorry and go to Accrington and bring a load of bricks from the kilns.

I was only there a few weeks. One day I came out and stopped in the main street, and I saw a notice in a shop window – motor mechanics wanted for a bus company. I thought, 'I'm in here.' I went in and asked to see the superintendent. I had a chat with him – you see I hadn't got a lot of experience, but I was taken on. I had to give a week's notice, and I left to work for this bus company as a mechanic there.

I look back nowadays, and I think of the Great War as a lot of political bull. There shouldn't be wars. That war was a lot of bloody political bull.

Alfred Anderson

Albert 'Smiler' Marshall

Henry Allingham

Cecil Withers

Alfred Finnigan

Fred Lloyd

Harry Patch

William Roberts

Thomas Kirk

Harold Lawton

George Rice

George Charles

Charles Watson

John Oborne

Kenneth Cummins

Ted Rayns

William Elder

George Hardy

Bert Clark

Bill Stone

Tom Kirk

Royal Navy · *Born* 13 January 1899, *died* 9 November 2004

I was born on 13 January 1899 in West Hartlepool. On my first birthday, I was presented by my uncles with a real steam engine of German make, with lots of lines. One of my earliest memories is of crawling after the engine, which was emitting a delicious smell of methylated spirit, oil and steam. On succeeding birthdays Uncles Tom, Peter and Harold always presented me with additional lines, signals and points.

I had two younger sisters, Mary and Nora. They were identical twins, so identical that no one outside the family could tell them apart. When we were children, the Pierrots were terribly important to us. They used to come every year and put up a small stage with a piano amongst the sand dunes at Seaton Carew where we lived. At the end of the performance they'd collect a few coppers from the children, in a bucket. They all called themselves 'Uncle' and I still remember their songs:

If I were Uncle Percy,
I would, I would, I would appear
On the end of the pier.
We all went to the shop to shelter from the rain,
We all had a lick of the raspberry stick,
And we all came out again.

In 1905 I remember a great adventure – a visit to London! I still remember the smell of leather seats and the swishing of the horses' tails as we went slowly along the mile of Station Road. I remember Father's remarks on the train as we neared Peterborough: 'Look out on the right and you may see a red Midland train racing us!' On the following day, we went to Brixton to pick up a tram into the City but the electrical supply from the cable sunk into the slit between the rails had somehow failed, and when the tram finally appeared, it was pulled by a horse. I had a vivid picture of Ludgate Hill and St Paul's but was not impressed by Drury Lane.

I was a nervous child. I remember a visit to Grandfather Hobson when he told me that on the previous night he had found a ladder propped up against a window. 'Evidently I disturbed a burglar,' he said. That night I woke up in the early hours to hear shuffling footsteps in my room. There was no electric light, only gas, so I shouted at the top of my voice, 'Don't move! I have a gun in my hand and I am going to shoot!' When I struck a light and lit the gas, I found a pile of leaves blowing about the floor.

In 1908 I remember staying with the Robsons, a wealthy family in Stockton. I arrived at about noon to hear that Sidney, the second son, had been locked in his bedroom with bread and water because he had tortured a cat. Meanwhile, Marjorie, Sidney's sister, was left

A portrait photo of Surgeon Lieutenant Tom Kirk,
probably taken during his posting to Portsmouth.

alone with me. She suggested that we should change clothes. Not
realising what this implied, I was starting to strip off when her mother
came in and marched me off to another room, where she gave me a
lecture on sex. Later that summer, when Sidney was again locked
up for some misdemeanour, a game of hide and seek was organised
and Marjorie disappeared. Some time later, she was found lying
beside a haystack in the arms of a naked farmhand.

Much later, Sidney wrote a very successful book entitled, *Working
My Way Round the World for £5*, which I was told was one long pack
of lies.

At around this time a strange and rather shameful episode
occurred. My close friend Jackie Bunting, later Colonel Bunting,
and I used to be rather jealous of the attraction the lovely golden
haired 'twinnies' roused in everyone they met. So we decided to
run away. We set off along Station Road, passed under the railway
bridge and arrived at Four Lane Ends. By that time we were cold,
hungry and miserable so we came home to be scolded by anxious
parents. I remember Jackie's sister, Kitty. She was lovely – I used to
gaze adoringly on her in church. Evidently, even at that age, I was
susceptible to female beauty.

In 1908, my father died. I went to the reception after his funeral
where I was reprimanded by Uncle Harold for kicking a football
about the lawn. 'Tom, please, NOT at a time like this!' Sadly, I realise
that I had seen so little of Father in the preceding year that his death
meant little.

In September of that year, I went to a boarding school in Lytham
– Seafield – run by an old family friend. He was determined that his
boys should see life from as many angles as possible, so we had expe-
ditions of all kinds. We took a cruise on the 'mud-hopper' up the

Ribble to Preston and we watched Preston North End, who were, at the time, the premier football team. The most exciting event was the first air display in 1909, where we watched Paul Chan sailing serenely above us in his Voisin biplane. The following year, Bleriot arrived in his biplane, having just made the first crossing of the Channel.

We concentrated a lot on sport, which is common, I suppose, to all boarding schools. I think I fancied myself as a future county cricketer. On wet days, the headmaster would spend hours with us in the gym bowling a tennis ball to a batsman wielding one cricket stump – excellent practice for playing a straight bat. At soccer I played left back. We won many games against bigger schools, possibly due to the headmaster's dubious advice – 'Go for the man, never mind the ball!'

On one occasion, when I was invited to Sunday dinner by the parents of a boy at Seafield, we threw mud from behind a hedge at the girls of Lowther College coming out of church in crocodile. We were spotted and soundly thrashed.

In 1912 I won a scholarship to Giggleswick – which relieved my mother of any further worry about school fees. This brought a telegram from Uncle Tom, 'Take two of your friends to Old Trafford to see Lancashire playing the Australians, at my expense.' We had a wonderful day, and we saw Reggie Spooner, our great hero, score a lot of runs. Unbelievably, Lancashire won the game by 24 runs.

Was boarding school a good thing? In spite of all the good aspects of Seafield, I must have decided no, because I was determined that if I ever had a son, I would not send him to a prep boarding school.

I was off to Giggleswick in 1912. What a joy after Seafield! A swim every morning in the cold swimming pool, Greek with dear

Tom Kirk, back row, second from the right, with colleagues at
Haslar Hospital in Gosport, 1917.

old H. M. F. Hammond, Latin with the fierce headmaster, R. N. Douglas – who was once a great cricketer and captain of Middlesex – maths with the genial E. G. Clark – 'The Bear' – French with Neumann, who took a fancy to me and gave me books until I was warned not to let him get too friendly. In those days nobody talked about homosexuality: bachelorship was a common occurrence. In fact, my final year at school was clouded by the Jepson Affair. Douglas Jepson was a keen cricketer who used to practise with me in the nets. I also shared a study with him and he developed a sort of 'pash' on me. Stupidly I did not nip it in the bud and he became jealous and possessive and estranged many of my friends. Hindsight tells me that this was homosexuality but at the time I was bewildered. He used to say, 'Can I come and stay with you and perhaps marry one of your sisters?' He did come too, but the twins would have nothing to do with him.

In 1914 we were all in the OTC, and I became a sergeant. With war looming we began to take ourselves very seriously under the command of the chaplain. At the end of the summer term, we took a train to Rugeley, Staffordshire. We were housed in tents – but war was now inevitable, so our tents were handed over to the army. We spent the last two nights in the open, which was no hardship. Whilst still dressed in my uniform, I took the train to Whitby and overheard a woman say, 'Surely they are not sending them so young?'

The war went on while I returned to school, and news was coming in of enormous casualties in Flanders, including some of my older school friends. Our OTC exercises were redoubled and I felt very proud when my section won the award for smartest section.

With the end of my last term approaching. I had a long inter-view with the headmaster during which he asked me why I had decided on medicine. I replied – I expect to his disappointment – that I had many relatives in medicine. I didn't tell him that Uncle Laurie had said to my mother, 'Put Tom in medicine and he'll be earning £400 a year in no time.' At least I was honest and never professed an earnest desire to save lives. When I left, the physics master said, in farewell, 'You'll be a rotten doctor, but you'll get away with it somehow.'

I think I came away from school a rather priggish little snob, convinced that Anglican Christianity and a fair knowledge of Latin and Greek were the essentials of life.

On the day I left school, I caught the Liverpool–Newcastle express. As the train entered Stockton Station, I saw Grandfather Hobson on the platform. He seemed very excited and put a lump of shell into my hand, saying, 'The Germans are in Hartlepool. This train can go no further.' But he was wrong – the train did go on, and before long we learned that German battlecruisers had bombarded Hartlepool and Scarborough. In Hartlepool there were over a hundred dead, but neither at Hartlepool nor Scarborough had the Germans done any serious structural damage, except by destroying some dwelling houses. What they *had* done was show up the deficiencies of our naval defences.

I sat the entrance exams for the College of Medicine – English literature, history, geography, French, Latin – but I don't think I did Greek. Later came an official letter: 'Passed', and written in pencil at the bottom 'and the university scholarship' – which meant £50 per annum for four years!

I was eighteen in January 1917 and I went to Fenham Barracks for a medical examination. I passed A1 and I was advised to submit my name to the Admiralty as surgeon probationer.

When we marched off to camp at Chapwell, breaking step on the Scotswood suspension bridge, I was in the senior squad – and the only one without a stripe. My only real accomplishment was in small-arms drill, which unfortunately resulted in my being picked out to take charge of the night guard. Somehow I allowed the fire to go out and I was reported to the major by the sergeant major who was furious: 'I hope he makes you dig latrines all tomorrow night!' I was told to report at 1600 hours to the major to get my punishment. At 1530 hours a telegraph boy cycled into the camp. It was a telegram for me, from the Admiralty. I showed it to the major, who hadn't even realised that I was on a charge. He read it, shook my hand and said, 'Well, I suppose we can't keep you any longer. Good luck.' And I walked out – giving a dismissive wave to the sergeant-major. I then had a few weeks to learn about wound-dressing in casualty at the Royal Victoria Infirmary.

Six weeks later, I got the call to Haslar Hospital in Gosport, where I found my old friend George McCoull. We were instructed in naval discipline – I was reproved for an incorrect shirt, and my jacket, made by civilian tailors in Grey Street instead of by Gieves, was considered 'old fashioned'. We spent our days on the wards, until our postings came up. McCoull went to a destroyer in the Dover Patrol, and I went to an L-Class destroyer, *Lydiard*, at Portsmouth.

Next day I reported aboard my ship. There was a crew of one hundred and five on the handsome, three-funnel destroyer. She'd been built on the Clyde and had a maximum speed of 29 knots.

I was made wardroom wine caterer – which was incongruous, because I'd promised my Uncle Harold not to touch strong drink until I was twenty-five. Apparently addiction to strong drink runs in our family. As a reward for this he paid the first premium of a life insurance. I stuck to my part of the bargain – but in retrospect it was all rather stupid, particularly as I had to pay all the subsequent premiums.

I was rather more astonished to find that I was the only medical officer in Portsmouth, with five destroyers and several P-boats to look after. This meant a series of medical inspections on ship after ship at which my incompetence was evident – to myself.

My ship was engaged chiefly on escort duty across the Channel. On one occasion, we were selected to test out the new experimental ASDIC – a device for spotting submarines. We took on board an admiral and while we were escorting two ships down the Channel at 5 knots, we spotted the conning tower of a submarine. I was on the bridge and the captain said, 'No time to drop depth charges. We ram!' Telegraphing for full speed, we waited for the crash, hanging on to any rail available. There was a dull thud and when we looked back at our wake, we could see the debris of the galley of a recently sunken steamer, complete with funnel. The result: a damaged propeller, and a refit – and two weeks' leave.

Our compasses on board were often defective. One morning, instead of sighting 'Number One buoy off Isle of Wight', we found ourselves off Newhaven and I was sent ashore to buy kippers.

America had now entered the war and we had the honour of escorting the first batch of American sailors from Southampton to Le Havre. We looked forward to the support of the US Navy but there were a lot of scornful remarks about the pictures of them crossing the Atlantic wearing life jackets.

One day, we received a signal – 'Proceed at once to replace *Mary Rose* on the Norwegian Convoy.' The *Mary Rose* had been sunk with all hands by German battlecruisers. Within hours we were underway, to the consternation of many officers who had wives in Portsmouth. Next day, we tied up at Port Edgar under the Forth Bridge.

During that winter of 1917 we made a lot of trips to Norway with the convoys. We were often a week out of port. Luckily the German fleet left us alone, although we had one alarm. We were called to action stations because there was the sound of heavy gunfire. Captain Lanford said, 'We're too slow to run away and our 4-inch guns are useless against capital ships. So we will ram the enemy in the hope that the convoy will get away.' This would mean goodbye to all of us. Luckily we soon learned that our battleship screens, always out of sight, were having battle practice. So complete anticlimax!

One of the great sights in the Forth was to see the K-boats come in after a cruise – these were steam-driven fleet auxiliary submarines with one massive 12-inch gun. They were difficult to handle and once there was havoc with collisions and a sinking, with great loss of life. On 31 January, Admiral Beatty took the Grand Fleet for an intensive exercise to ensure the fleet remained at full efficiency while waiting for the German High Seas Fleet to risk battle again. Nine K-boats sailed from Rosyth that evening, along with the battlecruiser squadrons. A U-boat was spotted, so all ships increased speed as they approached May Island, to offer a less easy target. But in the dark two small patrol boats wandered into the path of the K-boats. Turning to avoid them, the rudder of *K-14* jammed. She ended up broadside on to *K-22*, which, in the dark, saw her too late to avoid her and a serious collision left both submarines dead in the water. The light cruiser *Ithuriel* and three other K-boats had turned back to help. Unfortunately, the 12th Flotilla K-boats, led by the cruiser *Fearless*, were unaware of the accident ahead and ran straight into their sister flotilla. *Fearless* rammed *K-17*, and the submarine

Tom Kirk, aboard the L-Class destroyer *Lydiard*, whose operations included Channel escort duties and, in 1917, escort of Norwegian convoys from the base of Port Edgar on the Forth.

sank with all hands. Then *K-6* hit *K-4*, and nearly cut her in half. The two submarines sat locked together, but *K-7* was approaching fast astern. Spotting *K-6*, she just managed to avoid her, but was totally unaware of *K-4* lying across her path, and a further collision ensued. The second hit proved fatal for *K-4*, and she sank. Only nine men were pulled from the water. Over 100 men were lost that night.

This was off Kirkcaldy, where we were anchored – yet I saw nothing of it, and the news was never allowed out.

I was a good sailor and I had a theory that seasickness is largely in the mind. In one tremendous storm, I was peacefully sleeping in my swinging hammock when the officer of the watch came down and woke me. 'Aren't you sick? On the bridge we all are.' 'No,' I said, but as soon as he'd gone I had to get up and vomit. So much for my theory.

I often used to take the cable car from Leith into Edinburgh. Once Captain Lanford came with me. As we walked up Princes Street, he proclaimed, 'I don't like this street, Kirk. It's too full of HARLOTS!' That was a new word to me.

In May, I got word that I was to be released to continue my studies. I reported to a charming medical officer on the depot ship and returned my meagre stock of first-aid equipment and my drug cabinet, from which I'd so often dealt out pills and powders with little understanding of their properties.

Then it was back to Newcastle with a group of other returned surgeon probationers. We were still in uniform because we were in reserve. I went back to Stocksfield to live with my mother's younger sister Nora and her husband, John Naismith. After I qualified, I spent some months as an assistant, and worked as a locum, before going into partnership with Uncle Naismith in a practice in Barton-on-Humber in Lincolnshire.

In mid-autumn of 1919, I had become friendly with a very pretty staff nurse who came from Tow Law. On Christmas Eve, I paid her a visit. I asked a policeman, 'Can you direct us to Nurse Simpson?' 'You're two hours too late.' 'For what?' 'The wedding. She has married a sea captain.' I walked gloomily to catch a train. After that, my semi-official girlfriend was Catherine Morris Jones, whose death at the age of ninety-one I saw recorded in the *BMJ*. Then I met a young lady whose name I have sadly forgotten. She was a receptionist at the practice where I worked as a locum. We got on famously. My affair with her blossomed to the extent of an invitation to join her and her family in Torquay. This I did and I corresponded with her until my final letter announcing my engagement to Peggy Daniels, a letter which elicited a rather sad little note in reply.

Peggy Daniels was a Church High School girl from Newcastle. The school gave a dance and for the first time boys were admitted. I went with two other girls but I must confess my eyes were on Peggy D. I was invited to her parents' house, which soon became a second home to me. I proposed to her on the Town Moor, a highly unromantic setting, but she accepted. Her parents insisted on no marriage until she qualified from the College of Medicine. This led to a four-year engagement, devoid of anything approaching sensuality but buoyed by dreams of the joys of future matrimony.

Finally, in June 1925, I married her. We had a honeymoon touring in my little open two-seater Rover 9. This was before the days of helpful treatises on marital sex, which we could well have done with, as we were both very innocent. Perhaps there is much to be said for modern pre-marriage experimentation. We set up home in Whitecross Street – Uncle Naismith bought the house and I rented it from him. We had two children. In June 1927, our daughter June was born and two years later, Peter.

Medical work became more interesting. General medicine was beginning to become more scientific. One cure was anything but, however. A regular came to have his medicine bottle refilled. I handed it to him, saying, 'Here's your champagne.' To my surprise, we saw no more of him for six months. Meeting him, I stopped and asked, 'What's become of you?' 'I'm much better thanks to you.' 'Oh?' 'Yes, you told me to drink champagne so I went over to Hull and bought a bottle. My word, it were expensive, but it were worth it. I took a teaspoonful every day through the winter and I's a new man.'

I began hosting literary sessions at my house with Professor Billy Mayfield of Hull University. A dynamic young dentist called Brummitt became a regular. He also joined our badminton club and became a regular golfing partner of mine. He was skilful but there was something ruthless about him. I suffered from this when, in removing a perfectly good upper tooth in order 'to get a better look at a cavity in the next tooth', he used such force that he removed part of the floor of my left antrum with the result that there was an open passage from mouth to nose. Two days later, I had a high temperature and so I was taken to a nursing home in Hull. This was the days before antibiotics and my fever showed no signs of abating so they performed an operation. 'Brum', as we called him, came to see me and expressed remorse. I bore him no ill will, but the episode should have alerted me to the concealed violence in his nature.

A few years later, I was called to Brummitt's house to find him lying face down in a pool of blood. I cut away his tie and collar to find a four-inch gaping wound in his neck. Brummitt had killed his four-year-old son Terence and then cut his own throat. I put six stitches in Brummitt's neck. While I was doing this he started whispering, 'Tommy, Tommy, I have always thought the world of you. Let me die. I have killed my boy and nothing matters now. My wife has left me. Let me die.' We tied him to a stretcher and then I carried the sad little body of Terence to the bathroom, washed him, sponged out the bloodstained cot and laid him in it between towels. After that I went to see Brummitt's wife. The only comfort I could give her was that the boy must have died instantly.

I went to see Brummitt the next day in hospital. He was very weak but quite lucid and he insisted on telling me exactly how he'd done it – with a carving knife. He was very bitter about his wife, who, he said, had had an affair. Four days later, he seemed completely unaware of the seriousness of his crime. He was talking about applying for a 'school job' when he was better. At his subsequent trial, I appeared as a witness for the defence. Brummitt was found guilty but insane.

In 1939, I became very depressed by the evident pro-Hitler attitude of the Tory government. I had previously chaired a meeting to raise funds for the Republicans in Spain and there had been much popular support. Now, after Franco's success, came the next threat – Nazi Germany. After the German–Soviet pact, we abandoned any hope of peace. In spite of this, we decided to have our usual summer holiday at Yellow Sands Hotel on Harlyn Bay in Cornwall. It was on our return journey that we heard that war had been declared. The BMA decided that one member of our practice should be spared from joining the forces. Both my partner and I volunteered and they literally tossed a coin to decide who should go – and apparently they were happy to send him because I had served in the previous war.

During the war, I kept a diary. I kept it because I had little hope that we, or our way of life, would survive. The following are extracts from that diary:

18 May 1940

News so awful that I could not bear to write diary. Nor could we sleep. Danger of our forces becoming isolated in Belgium. Our broadcasts are so worded that people don't seem to realise how serious the situation is. They say, 'Marvellous – all those German planes brought down.'

20 May 1940

News glummer than ever. V. depressed and worried about how to behave under the Nazis.

21 May 1940

Is this the end? Germans taken Amiens and Arras and bombing Channel ports. 'Only a miracle can save us.' Carried on with my Barton First Aid course – 40–50 turned up, stolidly attending to the job – business as usual – no panic.

25 May 1940

Last night too depressed to write.

14 April 1941

(Bank Holiday) Lowest depths of depression. Germans have occupied Bardia and Sollum, bypassing Tobruk. I hear we are almost finished in Greece.

24 May 1941

Another ghastly shock. At 9 p.m. it was announced that the Hood had been sunk by the Bismarck. 'An unlucky shot exploded the magazine. Very few survivors.' What is wrong with our design of battlecruisers? Terribly afraid that my friend Hill was Commander on board Hood.

28 May 1941

Sudden reversal of fortune. Bismarck sunk! Four hundred miles off Land's End, torpedoed by aircraft from Ark Royal and finally finished off by the cruiser Dorsetshire. No word of survivors. BUT, we have lost two cruisers and four destroyers off Crete.

23 June 1941

It HAS happened. Yesterday at 5 a.m. Germany invaded Russia on a 2000-mile front. Excuse? 'To defend Europe against Bolshevism' and all that balls! Do they expect that they will get the support of America? If so, they've guessed wrong. Winston says, 'I hate Communism but will support Russia in every way possible.' Roosevelt follows with almost as strong a statement. Bernard Shaw says, 'The news is almost too good to be true.' Most people think that the Germans will have a walk-over, but McCredy and others on the left think differently.

31 May 1942

Sunday. Still feeling exhausted after a terrible night. Was out until 2 a.m. and had just got to bed when Jim S. phoned to say that Barrow had

been badly blitzed and was in flames. I was wanted at once. Feeling like
death, I tried to pull myself together. Terrible devastation. Nobody
seemed to know where I was wanted. A huge crater where the Tongs'
house and shop had been, and a girl was reported missing. I fell down in
the mud and dumped my two heavy bags beside a yard door. Behind
the door I found the girl's body, terribly mangled and quite dead. Thos.
Till (Warden) was knocked down by the Fire Engine and had to be
splinted up. To add to the misery, the rain poured down in torrents. Only
other casualty that I had to deal with was Miss Larder (an elderly
woman) who was badly burned on face and hands, trying to put out
incendiaries.

7 May 1943

Great surprise. Tunis and Bizerta fell tonight. How long will the enemy
hold out on Cap Bon? And how many will get away? In the Caucasus,
things are going badly for the Germans . . .

19 May 1943

Am I getting slack with this diary because the war news improves? I
started it with the idea that someday only this diary would be left to
reveal the truth about one small family in the days before our civilisation
perished. Now we have hopes of survival. The exciting news is that,
instead of hanging on for weeks as we expected, the whole Axis army in
North Africa has capitulated.

27 July 1943

I have become an aircraft pilot (sort of)! On Sunday at Cob Hall I
arranged with Jake Kennard to meet him at Elsham on Tuesday. It was
cloudy and thundery when I got there at 2.30, wearing Home Guard

uniform. Jake took me round the airfield in a staff bus, visiting bomb-bays containing huge shapeless 4000- and 8000-lb bombs. Then to see the girls packing parachutes and finally to be offered the choice of a Lancaster or his own little Miles Magister. I chose the latter. He explained to me the instruments and, as soon as we were in the air, he said, 'Now she's all yours,' and held his hands above his head. I was staggered. After climbing steadily I tried a left bank and turn, to which he said, 'Very good.' There was no horizon, only a haze, and it was hard to tell if one was climbing or dropping. Gradually I learned to watch the revs and judge by that. He said, 'Put her into a dive.' The tiniest movement forward of the joystick put us into a dive, and I prayed that she would pull out. She did. After some level flying I had no idea of direction until Jake said, 'You'll soon be over the North Sea. Better turn. We don't want to visit Germany.' I spotted an airfield below and thought we were back where we'd started. No, it was Kirmington. I felt it was time I handed over, so that I could concentrate on map-reading. Jake then took us low over Barton and at tree-top level up the Ancholme to beyond Briggs. Barton looked quite lovely from the air, with its churches and many trees. We landed easily on a side-road at Elsham and I said goodbye to the charming little open monoplane.

28 September 1943

Jake is missing. Last night our planes were over Hanover. All came back except one. I was somehow uneasy about Jake, and it was no surprise when I got back to hear that the padre had been over. I walked back from Cob Hall with Joan. She said, 'Perhaps the war will be over soon. I am sure Jake is a prisoner. What a reunion we will have.' I could have cried.

Tom Kirk, third man from the left, with hospital
staff at Gosport.

24 March 1944

Work as heavy as ever. I asked George Gilmour to visit Miss Chapman,
who had been in bed for many years and has had monthly visits from
me. It was the first time he'd seen her. She said, 'Who are you?' and fell
back. When he put his stethoscope on her, he realised she was dead. They
fetched Mr Chapman, her nephew, a farmer, and his comment was,
'Good. Dr Kirk should have sent you years ago.'

When at last the war was over, we were pretty exhausted from
overwork and lack of sleep so we took the earliest opportunity to
fly to Dublin to consume delicious food, which entranced us after
our years of semi-starvation.

After the war, and the formation of the NHS, I continued in
practice. We were allowed to take private patients but decided not
to and so got rid of financial doctor–patient concerns.

It was never uncommon to be compelled to certify maniacal
subjects and send them away under police escort. One violent young
man tried to throw me out of a bedroom window and his last words
as we overpowered him were, 'When I get out I'll kill you . . . ' Many
months later, at the end a long Saturday-night surgery, I recognised
the man sitting alone in the waiting room. Everybody else had gone
home. Nervously I called him in and he sat down. 'Now, Doctor,' he
began and paused. 'I think I'm getting a sore throat. Will you have a
look?'

On another occasion, I was called to see a man found dead in a
barn. I was met by the farmer, who showed signs of distress. 'What
happened?' I asked. 'I can hardly bear to tell you,' he said. 'Jim had
been a bit depressed lately and this morning he said, "I think I'll put
an end to it," but I thought he was joking so I said, "Well get on with

it but shut the door."' Hearing a shot, the farmer had gone in and found Jim with his head blown off. This conversation was not recorded at the inquest.

I reached retiring age on 13 January 1964 but I continued working for three months. Peggy and I found a house in Stocksfield. It was a semi-detached property with half an acre of garden, and we bought it for about £5,000. So began what turned out to be the happiest sixteen years of our lives. We joined the Stocksfield players and were very soon given parts – and later, when the director moved away, I took over from her and produced a number of plays, including *Hay Fever*, *The Constant Wife* and *The Playboy of the Western World*. I had already written some plays in the 1950s, one of which was accepted by the BBC. In 1966, my book, *Back to the Wall*, an adventure book for older children, was accepted for publication by Faber and Faber. The following year, Faber published my next book, *The River Gang*. I look back on the sixties as a cheerful time – apart from the Cuban crisis – Swinging London, the Beatles. Certainly it was for us.

On 15 June 1974, Peggy and I celebrated forty-nine years of perfect marital bliss. At the same time, I heard that my sister Nora had died in hospital in Liverpool. Peggy drove me to the station and I caught a train to Liverpool, where I attended Nora's funeral. When I returned home, the phone was ringing. I was told that Peggy had died peacefully in her sleep.

We had become very fond of the Penny family, who lived opposite, and after Peggy's death they insisted that I accompany them on all their holidays, one year to Tuscany, another to the Pyrenees. I have kept very busy on various duties – SICA Council, the Day Centre, Meals on Wheels, weekly meetings of the Stocksfield Singers – at some of whose concerts I have been the only bass. I have been presenting 'Northern Arts' and because I have felt uncomfortable badgering people to buy tickets to productions, I have found that the one way to ensure a reasonable audience has been to invite them to what became known as the 'Kirk Orgy' after the performance.

I am often teased about my 'girlfriends'. I find women attractive to look at and to listen to. They are more down to earth than men, which may explain why the best present-day novelists are women. When I went to a friend's memorial service in Winterton, I ate lunch with my daughter June and her husband Bill at the Humber Bridge Hotel. It was a most sumptuous place with comfortable chairs and log fires. I expressed my admiration to one of the busy young waitresses and Bill shouted, 'Stop talking up that young lady and tell me what you want to drink!' to which the girl replied, 'Don't take him away, I'm enjoying him.' At the end of the meal, as I stood up to pay, the waitress said, 'What about a kiss?' I was delighted to oblige – to the astonishment of a crowd of strangers.

It surprises me today that local doctors take no interest in local events. What a contrast to the old days. Relationships seems to have become very impersonal: the computer rules. Nevertheless, from letters from old friends, I get the impression that doctors still do a lot of visiting. What strikes me about general practice today is the enormous fee required to be paid to the Medical Defence Union. If I were starting in medicine today, I should be terrified. Also it has become so submerged in biochemistry that I can no longer read my weekly BMJ with understanding or enjoyment.

Recently, I read an eighteenth-century warning: 'Old men should resist the temptation to pontificate.' My temptation is the reverse: to attack all pontificators. My earliest memories are of the closing stages of the Boer War – my heroes were Lord Roberts, Baden-Powell and, above all, Sir George White – 'Big Dodge' – the defender of Ladysmith. The Kirk clan was militantly patriotic; the Boers were little better than the Zulus – 'breeds without the law'. After that came a build-up of anti-German feeling that led to the slaughter of the First World War. Today, I vote Liberal because I abhor the two extremes, Right and Left. Thatcherism produced a violent money-grabbing public, but here in Stocksfield, where busy housewives spend their short hours of leisure running Sunday schools, Scouts, singing weekly with the choir, I feel fortunate. Here I sit, over a hundred years old, a typical *Guardian* reader in a stone house, set in a wild half-acre of garden. A friend of mine said to me recently, 'You are lucky to live in such peaceful surroundings.' Very true.

Harold Lawton

Cheshire Regiment, attached to 4th East Yorkshire Regiment
Born 27 July 1899, *died* 24 December 2005

I was born in the Potteries, at Burslem, near Stoke-on-Trent and I had my early education at the Church School. I was in their infants' school when I was three. It was close to my home and I went with my two sisters who were at the same school.

When I was about ten, I met and fell in love with a little girl of seven called Bessie. On the day that she and I met, my mother and her mother were talking, and they told us to go and have a walk along an interesting little bit of canal. It was all quite proper and while our two mothers were doing what they wanted to do, my little girl and I would go walking. It was marvellous, she was lovely – and a very long time later we were married and were happy together for fifty-eight years until she died in 1991.

When I was eleven I started secondary school. My two sisters were learning French as part of their student teacher training and I started to learn it too. It particularly attracted me and I really took to it. When my family moved from the Potteries to North Wales, I didn't follow them straight away; I stayed to get on with my schooling at Newcastle-under-Lyme. Then after that I went to Rhyl Grammar School, where I was in the Army Cadets. When I was eighteen, I was called up and joined the Royal Welch Fusiliers, before transferring to the Cheshire Regiment – which was just a matter of changing the buttons.

I went for training in Yarmouth. I was a good shot, for one thing. On 24 June 1916 the German navy bombarded the town. They moved past us very quickly, firing on our billets. I don't think anybody was killed. Later on, Jerry got an opportunity to send something a bit bigger over, and he did in the shape of a Zeppelin airship, which dropped bombs on the town.

I was posted to the front in France but it was all very chaotic. Regiments were being amalgamated and you didn't really know from day to day where you belonged. In December 1917 we were attached to the 4th East Yorkshire Regiment and we went to Béthune. The line hardly moved and all I can really remember is the noise, the cold and the fact that we were hungry and seemed to have permanently wet feet. In April of the following year, as the Germans were on the offensive near Armentières, a Portuguese battalion was overrun and I ended up with six Durham Light Infantrymen in a trench. We had to dig a temporary line with hand tools. We were completely cut off. We held on for as long as we could, but we had no supplies of ammunition or food for three days and, when the waves of Jerries came over, we had no option but to surrender. They took us prisoner and we were put in a 'cage' for a few days. We were then transported to Lille, to a prison they referred to as 'The Black Hole' because so many of its prisoners died of disease. The flu epidemic

Army Cadet Harold Lawton, age sixteen, at Rhyl
Grammar School. Called up at the age of eighteen
in 1917, he joined the Royal Welch Fusiliers
before transferring to the Cheshire Regiment.

was rife, and killed huge numbers there. The prison was a fort that had originally been built by the French. We were all put into one great, massive room. It was absolute hell. There were shelves on the walls and men lay on these shelves wherever they could. Some of the men had been hurt and some hadn't. I'd never known anything like it.

We weren't there for long but it seemed like a very long time indeed. They moved us by cattle trucks to Westphalia, where I was sent temporarily to a camp in Limburg, then on to Minden. Here, I was given a job peeling potatoes. The prisoners were divided into two groups – the better educated and the others. Fortunately, I was in the former group, which was given much lighter duties. The others were put to hard manual labour. After a while I was moved off to a much bigger camp, which, I must say, was well run. I was there when the Armistice was signed. We'd been expecting it.

In that last camp, there was one man who had lived very near to me in England. Twice, he tried to escape. He was a very intelligent man and he had a jolly good try. On both occasions, he managed to get into a motorboat on the water surrounding the camp, but each time he was spotted and brought back. Strange to say, he was liked by the Germans. The two Germans officers who were in charge said, 'You're a nice chap, aren't you, going off like that? We keep having to come after you, to bring you back again. What on earth do you think you're doing?' Effectively they told him that they didn't mind his trying to escape so long as he didn't use up too much petrol in the attempt! The camp commandant said, 'I've got to punish you in some way,' which he did. It was an odd business, because the two German officers in charge were the fine type of German. They knew all about army life and they understood that you were expected to try to escape. It was all a rather cock-eyed arrangement, particularly as we thought that they were going to shoot him. Some of the German officers we came across later on were not quite as sporting.

In our quarters at the camp we had some things that were sent to us and that we were allowed, by law, to have. These included some red handkerchiefs. One of the German officers came round on one occasion and he said, 'I wonder whether you'd be very, very kind – it would be a tremendous help to me if I could have some of your red handkerchiefs.' He wanted them to stitch together to make a flag. We gave him nine red handkerchiefs and he stitched them all together. We saw the finished flag flying from the flagpole.

My escaping friend was the first man out after the Armistice, and I think he was the first man back in England. I saw him again after the war. When I was released, I travelled by train to Holland and sailed from Rotterdam to Cromer. We sailed in a captured German ship and the captain told us that there were still mines in the North Sea. He said that if we were hit, we were to assemble on deck, if it was still there, then scramble down the ropes, provided they were still there, and then take our chances in the freezing, mined water. I'll never forget how relieved we were when we finally dropped anchor in Cromer. I arrived back in Rhyl in December 1918, only to be told that I'd been demobbed too early, so I was sent back to the army, where I was given an office job filling in discharge papers!

When I arrived home, I was shown a notice from the *Rhyl Journal* of 8 June 1918: 'After having been reported missing since 10 April, Private Harold Walter Lawton, son of Mr and Mrs Lawton, West Kinmel Street, is now known to be a prisoner in Germany. A postcard from Limburg, dated 14 April, states that he is quite sound, but not likely to remain at Limburg long. Pte Lawton, who is not yet 19 years old, proceeded to the front at Easter with a draft for the East Yorkshire Regiment, and was in action almost immediately. Prior to joining up last August, he was an officer of the Rhyl Intermediate School Cadets.'

I carried on with my French studies after the war, obtaining an MA (Honours) degree at the University of Wales at Bangor in 1921, followed by a fellowship in 1923. I then went to Paris and read for a doctorate in Latin and French Renaissance Literature at the Sorbonne. I obtained a double first degree and stayed on at the Sorbonne as a junior lecturer for two years. Paris in the twenties was an extraordinary place and I was, indeed, fortunate to have been there. I spent much time in Montmartre amongst the artists and in the Latin Quarter browsing through the fabulous book stalls.

Rather reluctantly, I returned to England and, in 1930, became a lecturer in French and modern languages at the University College of Southampton. I was also the first warden of New Hall from 1930 to 1933. In the early 1930s the then Archbishop of Canterbury asked me to transcribe the handwritten diaries of Lord Gladstone, who was prime minister from 1880 to 1885 and again from 1892 to 1894. The diaries had been given into the safe-keeping of the Church and were housed in Lambeth Palace. They contained, amongst many other things, sensitive material about Gladstone's relationship with and opinion of Queen Victoria. Gladstone's handwriting was extremely difficult to read and what I thought was to be a small job turned into an enormous task. The job was to be carried out in great secrecy during the university vacations.

I had, by great good fortune, met my childhood sweetheart, Bessie, again and in a very short time we became engaged to be married. As the work on the Gladstone diaries became more onerous

Harold Lawton (far left) with comrades in the Cheshire Regiment, pictured during training at Great Yarmouth in 1915.

and, as I was not a typist, I asked the Archbishop if Bessie could help me. Although she was a nurse, her typing was much better than mine. I told the Archbishop that I could trust her implicitly and he agreed.

Bessie and I were married in 1933 and our eldest son, David, was born in 1935 followed by our only daughter, Elisabeth, in 1937. In that year, when Southampton University College was given its charter and became a fully fledged university, I was made the first professor of modern languages. Our second son, Graham, was born in 1939 just before war broke out.

When the Second World War was declared, I joined the police force as a special constable to 'do my bit'. I spent many hours on patrol in the dock area and 'Below Bar' in Southampton. When the bombing of Southampton became too intense, I was able to find other accommodation for my wife and three children in Liss, a small village about thirty-five miles outside the city. I continued with my work at the university and also began a series of lectures and talks to British troops and airmen about the French people, their customs, their style of dress and their language. During the First World War, many of our soldiers failed to grasp the French mentality and the idea of these talks was to make sure that no such misunderstandings arose again. My audiences ranged from a handful of troops in a room to more than a thousand in a large theatre. Some of the talks were aimed at Allied infiltrators, in the hope that they would be able to operate successfully when dropped by the SOE in France. As a result of these activities, it was later discovered that my name was on a Nazi 'wanted' list. The Germans were very thorough and had categorised a large number of Britons according to their position, their abilities and their likely usefulness after a German conquest.

A list of names had also been drawn up of people who would be 'seen to' if Hitler ever ruled Britain. My name was on it.

After the war I became dean of the Faculty of Arts at Southampton University. In 1950, I was appointed professor of French at the University of Sheffield. I later became warden of Ranmoor Hall of residence and pro-vice-chancellor of the University. I stayed in that post until I retired in 1964.

Bessie and I had bought a holiday home in Rhosneigr, on Anglesey, and we lived there permanently after retirement for fifteen very happy years. I spent many hours there beachcombing, walking and sketching. We used to travel overseas quite often. In 1979, we moved to Kent to be near my daughter and her husband, Jeremy, and finally moved with them to Rutland in 1987. Very sadly Bessie died in 1991 followed only two years later by my eldest son, David. In 2000, my younger son, Graham, also passed away.

In 1999 I became Chevalier, Légion d'honneur – an honour bestowed by the French on all surviving veterans of the Great War. It is a great honour and one which gives me enormous pleasure. I have always loved the French people, their language and, indeed, their cuisine!

At the age of 105, I can now only sit and think about an extraordinary life, which I feel very privileged to have lived.

George Rice

1/5th Battalion, Durham Light Infantry
Born 18 June 1897, *died* 17 September 2005

I was born in Stockton-on-Tees on 18 June 1897 and left school at fourteen. I first worked for WH Smith, selling books at the railway station, and I enjoyed the work but felt it would be better to do an apprenticeship, so I trained as a coppersmith. I later changed my job and became a sheet-metal worker and metal model maker. I joined the Territorial Army at seventeen. We had a TA training camp every year and in 1914 our annual training camp was in Wales at Deganwy near Llandudno. It turned out to be like a holiday. One day during a break some of us climbed a local hill to have a good view of the surroundings. When we reached the top we heard a bugle sound and saw a lot of the lads running about below. I wondered what was going on and when we returned to camp we were told that the war had started. We were all shocked when they ordered us back to Stockton-on-Tees on 3 August. Nobody talked as we marched to the railway station to go back to our barracks.

Shortly afterwards, most of the battalion was shipped out to

George Rice, pictured at his wedding to Elsie in 1927.

France but because of my coppersmith and sheet-metal skills, I was ordered to Wallsend to help with the manufacture of ships' pipes. I worked in a factory alongside civilians. Army regulations required me to wear my white-belted khaki uniform and I stood out a bit in the factory surroundings. Now and again those of us on this special assignment would march round the locality to maintain our military training.

Eventually, I was called up to go to the front in 1917 and transferred from the Durham Light Infantry to the Duke of Wellington's Regiment. They put me on a refresher course – to remind me how to kill, so to speak, where I was trained on the Lewis Gun. There were two of us working together. As the Number One it was my job to fire the machine gun and the other man was detailed to load the gun and put it right if it went wrong. On completing this training we sailed to Boulogne early in 1918 and from there my battalion was posted to Havrincourt in northern France.

This was the front line. The Germans were halfway into France and we were chasing them back. We were moving a thousand yards at a time, leapfrogging in the direction of Germany. The fighting was incessant and ferocious. The trenches were horrible and wet and cold.

On one occasion, my section had fought intensely all day to capture a commanding ridge. We secured it and started to dig in. The 'old sweats' in the unit, young men in their twenties, said, 'Be careful because Jerry will counter-attack almost immediately before we can dig in.' Sure enough, minutes later the enemy came at us from nowhere. They charged with bayonets raised, screaming wildly to demoralise us. They were so close that they weren't using their rifle-sights – they were shooting openly over them. The lieutenant in charge standing right next to me was shot dead. I had no time to react and I could not wedge the two front legs of my Lewis gun into the ground. Those around me desperately tried to help to secure them as the Germans ran nearer. When the gun was finally stabilised, and the Germans were almost on top of us, I pulled the trigger and eight Germans fell dead. I didn't have to aim, they were so near. They ran in a line into my bullets.

Whatever I thought about it later, at the time it was just my job as a soldier. They were the enemy and they were to be ruthlessly fought. It was them or us; feelings didn't come into it.

Another time, we had spread out down a lane, alongside a railway embankment only just high enough to give us some cover but with a good view of the line. There was a lull in the battle noise. Obviously we kept extremely quiet. Deathly silent. Then in the moonlight a lone German soldier came into view, patrolling the railway line. Although we were under orders to hold fire, someone in our sector couldn't resist taking a shot at this lone man. At once, this triggered a massive discharge of arms along the line. The German soldier, facing certain death, went into a panic. He zig-zagged, ducked and dived to avoid the hail of bullets. Suddenly, one of the more sensitive among us called out in a very loud voice, 'Give him a chance, chaps!' The firing ceased and the sentry ran off. We all felt very emotional and strangely moved.

On a lighter note, but to show how jumpy we always were, I walked out one night in my soft shoes, unable to sleep because of a toothache, heading for the latrines. But there was somebody in there. As I went in, my soft shoes were noiseless; poor devil, he jumped out of his skin, no doubt thinking I was a German. Such was the constant fear.

The fighting was relentless right up to 11 November. After the Armistice, my unit was released into Namur in Belgium for a few days of celebration before returning to Havrincourt. There, because of overcrowding in the billets, I had to sleep in a water-filled shell hole. As a result, I became seriously ill with trench fever and was taken to hospital whilst the rest of my battalion returned home. I had to stay behind in France to recuperate, eventually being taken by ship and train to a hospital in Newcastle where I was demobbed.

My experiences in the war made me grow up very quickly.

At the age of twenty-two, I moved south from Stockton-on-Tees looking for work, found a job at the Austin Motor Company at Long-bridge and moved into digs at Harborne, Birmingham. The landlord was a very devout Christian. We talked a lot together and it was largely down to him that I was converted. This gave me a new direction and changed my life completely. Some time later when more settled, my mother and sister moved down to Smethwick in the Midlands and it was whilst staying with them that I met my wife Elsie. We married when I was thirty, which was quite late, delayed from normal I suppose because of the war. Anyhow, we went on to have four lovely sons. Elsie did me proud!

Later, I became a lay preacher. Our four sons were raised in the Christian faith and their upbringing was centred on the Gospel Hall in Northfield. Unfortunately we have lost two of our sons through illness but David, the oldest, lives in Hertfordshire and Alvan, my youngest, lives all the way up in Scotland. I remember when Alvan was born, all the family gathered around the bed to choose his name. We got out the Bible concordance and scanned the names. Unanimously, we chose Alvan. Our family nickname for him used to be 'Genesis 36:23'. At present, we have ten grandchildren and ten great-grandchildren.

During the Second World War, familiar circumstances revisited me. I was again working on war production, this time in Coventry on special devices fitted to Halifax bombers to counteract the barrage balloon menace. Although my life had completely changed since I had been a mere lad in the trenches, my old feelings seemed to return during the many German bombing raids. On one particular day, I travelled from my home in Northfield to Coventry for my work. It was the morning after the terrible blitz. All my youthful memories returned with a vengeance as I clambered through the horrible devastation of that day. Facing the carnage and calls for help, it was impossible to get to work that day. I returned home many, many hours late in a very distressed state.

However, we always look for lighter moments, don't we? My daily trip of eighteen miles each way from Birmingham to Coventry suffered from continual travel disruption. Such a distance meant I left home very early and returned very late at night, often when the rest of the family were in bed. In those days we had a sort of cooking range and one night I returned home tired to find a dish of food warming in the oven. I tucked into this vegetable-type stew – only to discover next morning it was a preparation for the chickens we kept during the war. I never lived that down with the family. Fortunately I hadn't congratulated the chef!

For a few years before retirement, I spent a most enjoyable part of my working life working for Joseph Lucas, the automotive lamp manufacturers in Birmingham. Having had a lifetime in various hectic production workshops wearing overalls and workcoats, I was given a white coat and my own dedicated workstation, well lit and

George Rice, like many men whose lives were put on hold because of the war, married relatively late at the age of 30.

with excellent tools. Although we still had deadlines to meet, the normal pressures of work were replaced by an emphasis on hand-skill and craftsmanship. I had arrived in the Prototype and Precision Model Making Department. We fashioned the metal and built the products by hand. One of my proudest achievements was to hand-make the shield-bezel for Birmingham's coat of arms for the roof of the Lord Mayor's official car.

I retired late, at the age of seventy-one. My wife and I had always loved the Isle of Wight. We had spent many happy family holidays there and we always said it would be nice to live there – so we did! We were there for thirteen years before realising we were getting very old so moved back to Birmingham to an Anchor Homes place at Edgware Court, Edgbaston. This was a warden-controlled scheme which Elsie and I enjoyed for several years. We had our own flat in the complex and had a fair amount of independence but meals were provided. We made so many friends there. Eventually, as Elsie's health deteriorated and she started needing more care, it was recommended that we move to one of their other homes equipped with round-the-clock nursing service, so in 1994 we moved to Tandy Court, Kings Heath in Birmingham. Unfortunately, over time, Elsie's health worsened and she became confined to a wheelchair. She passed away on 7 January 1997. We had been married sixty years. I was very lost and lonely at first and had to move to a new single flat in the same building. The staff were very good and helped me through the grieving process. I still think of Elsie every day.

I have been fortunate in my life not to have suffered much ill health. Even now, I feel good in myself and enjoy mixing with the other residents. Occasionally I take my mouth organ to the lounge and give them a little tune, which they all seem to enjoy. I learnt the mouth organ when I was ten years old and it's always been useful. Even when I was in the trenches I used to play it. When you're young, you can pick up anything and it sticks. For years now my electric keyboard has given me much pleasure. It has to be kept plugged in so that I can play it whenever the feeling takes me; friends say it keeps me alive!

I never used to talk very much about my wartime experiences. I was very young at the time and so much has happened to me since, but now that there are so few veterans left, everybody wants to speak to me.

Even though I still enjoy life, I sometimes feel as though I've had enough. I know that, one day, Jesus will call and take me to Elsie.

George Charles

7th Battalion, Durham Light Infantry
Born 2 October 1899, *died* 10 December 2004

I was born on 2 October 1899 in South Shields, one of seven. I had four brothers and two sisters. I was five when I first went to school – we used to walk there.

My father worked as a coal-hawker and when I left school at fourteen I became an apprentice at Gray's Engineering. It was in 1917 that I joined the Durham Light Infantry at Rossendale – but before that I remember the Germans bombing Hartlepool. A lot of people were killed and it was very frightening.

We did some training, then we were shipped out to France. I was a private when we moved up to the front and went into the trenches. It was filthy and cold – and we lived on bully beef and biscuits. We used to live for the letters we got from home – I got letters from my parents and I wrote back to them.

We relied on our comrades – and I lost a lot of friends I had met during our training.

A studio photo of George Charles, standing, with his father.

The fighting was bloody, but there were moments of humour. One time there was a group of five of us who got separated from the main battalion. We found a deserted farmhouse and checked it for Germans. We didn't find any and, well, we'd had no food for about thirty-six hours, so we found a chicken outside and killed it. We lit a fire in the fireplace and started to cook it – but sparks and smoke went up the chimney and alerted the enemy – and as soon as they got our range, we became a target. There were explosions all around us and we had to abandon our lunch and clear out.

Another frightening moment was when I was on my own on sentry duty. I heard this rustling in the trees behind me, and I thought I'd had it. Then something knocked into my back and I turned round to find a horse that had got loose. It helped to have a sense of humour to get you through.

When I came back I returned to Gray's and finished my apprenticeship and in 1923 I married my sweetheart from before the war – Annie-Marie, who worked as an embroiderer in Fowler's Department Store. We went to live in Beccles, where we brought up our three daughters – they still come to see me, but none of them looks like their mother.

In the Depression, ships we worked on were laid off, so in 1929 I became a surface worker at Horton Colliery, where I played the euphonium in the band. Then later the family helped me become a foreman engineer in the bottling store of the new brewery, Aitchison's Ales. In 1937 I moved to Thompson's Brewery at Deal as assistant bottling manager and to Dutton's Brewery in Blackburn in 1940. During the war, in 1942, I moved to Courage at Tower Bridge, where I eventually became bottling manager and stayed there until I retired in 1964.

My wife died in 1991, and I lived on my own until going to a home in 1999. I've had a healthy life, really. I never smoked – not even during the war. I didn't drink then either, but I like a drink now. I was recently sent a brew of porter which was originated at the start of the twentieth century – so it's as old as me.

All my working life I was an engineer, but in my spare time I always enjoyed gardening. I had a lovely garden – especially after I retired. I grew roses, chrysanthemums – all sorts.

I've had a remarkable and happy life – but like a lot of people, I never liked to talk about the war when I got back. People had lost fathers, sons and husbands and we didn't see anything to celebrate. We in the Durhams lost a lot of men – and now I think I'm the last of them from that war. It was all such a complete waste of lives.

Charles Watson

11 Squadron, Royal Flying Corps
Born 16 November 1899, *died* 1 January 2005

I was born on 16 November 1899 in Romsey in Hampshire. My father was away in the Boer War when I was born, and he didn't see me until I was about three. He was with the Somerset Light Infantry and when he came back we went to the barracks at Taunton. My brother was born in Exeter and so was my sister. My brother died two or three years ago. He was a radio officer on the Cunard liners, so he spent his life sailing all round the world. He went to Australia, New Zealand – all round the world. My sister stayed at home and looked after my mother.

When I was small, my pocket money was a farthing a fortnight. We used to go to Mrs Mallion's little shop and she'd have a piece of liquorice and tear it down in strips – and if there were two of us, we'd tear it up and have half each. She used to make her own sweets and we got four if we had a halfpenny. She used to screw up a piece of paper with four sweets in. I was five when I went to the infants' school in Devizes – the three of us went together. I remember these rows of houses and we used to get a piece of string, and we'd tie it round two door handles next to each other – then we'd knock on both doors and run across the road. One person would come out and pull the door, then the other person next door would pull their door. We were on the other side of the road laughing at them. They'd shout, 'We'll get you!' But they never did.

My father was a regular soldier – a captain in the Somerset Light Infantry. He fought in South Africa, in the Transvaal, at the relief of Ladysmith, in the Orange Free State, Tupelo Heights and in the Cape Colony. For his service there he was awarded the 1901–2 South African Medal and long service and good conduct medals. Then he came home, and twelve years later the First World War started, and he went to France. He went out some time before I did – I was only fifteen when the war started.

While we were in Taunton I was very young and my education was very bitty. We moved about a lot. When my father went to France, we went to Portland, then back to Taunton, then to Exeter and later Devizes. When we were based at the barracks in Taunton we used to see the wounded men coming back, so I had some idea of what might await me if I joined the army. I used to see the men before they went to the war, then I'd see them coming back – one with his leg off, one with his arm off.

I finished my schooling at the County Boys' School in Cambridge. Then everybody over the age of eighteen was called up for the army. So, when I was eighteen I told my father I wanted to join the Royal Flying Corps, and he said, 'You're a bloody fool. They shoot 'em down like shooting pigeons in a field.' But I said, 'I don't mind. I'd like to have a go.' So he let me go. I went to the place where we had to

Sergeant Charles Watson, 11 Squadron, Royal Flying Corps, photographed in 1918. Although his father, fighting on the ground below in the trenches, had warned him of the perils of flying, Watson survived to serve with the Army of Occupation in Germany after the Armistice.

join up and they fitted us with an ordinary army uniform. We attended medical examinations at the Hotel Cecil in London, and a number of men were rejected.

During my training, I was taught aerial gunnery and photography and I spent part of the time billeted on the seafront at Hastings. After that, I went out to join 11 Squadron based at Remains near Audi-le-Château on the Western Front, as an observer. I remember the day I arrived. I was billeted in a tent on the edge of the airfield and I was very tired, wet, hungry and homesick.

Right from the beginning, while we were flying over the front there was a lot of heavy fighting on the ground. We could see all the men being shelled down below and I used to think of my father. He was down there in the mud and trenches and I used to look over the side of the aircraft at all the fighting and think, 'I'm better off up here than he is down there.' But he managed to survive. He had always said, 'Don't go in aeroplanes. You'll be killed!' but we both got through to the end. He was about eighty-nine when he died.

In the aircraft we'd wear a silk vest and woollen pants and woollen socks and shirt, then our uniform – and on top of that a flying suit. I was the Lewis gunner in this Bristol F2B fighter. I sat in the second seat, facing the tail. I used to get a grip on the gun to point it up and down and around. I'm not sure if I ever shot anything down – once you got into a fight, you didn't know if you were going down or up. When we were in the air, I'd see the enemy coming. They'd always come at you from the back. Never from the front. If you were lucky they missed you. I also had to take photos leaning over the side for reconnaissance – I had a semi-automatic camera fitted to the floor inside the cockpit.

We got in quite a few fights over France. On one occasion, on

9 August 1918, which was the day after the Allies launched a massive attack on the Western Front, I got shot – at least, my engine got shot. We were in a Bristol escorting these DH4s on a bombing raid on a bridge and we were at about 1600 feet when a hail of bullets shattered our fuel tank. The pilot, Sergeant Hutt, was temporarily blinded by petrol fumes, so I fitted the spare joystick and I dived for the nearest cloud. The engine stopped and we were losing height and I had no idea whether we were over our lines or enemy lines. I looked around for somewhere to land and I spotted a cornfield. There was a ditch across the blooming field and we hit the ditch and over we went. I got a bump on my head but my mate, the pilot, was knocked unconscious. I wasn't too bad so I released Sergeant Hutt and then I saw a group of soldiers running towards me. I still didn't know whether they were friendly or not so I released the Lewis Gun from its mounting and waited in the ditch. When the soldiers arrived, they shouted at me in French and I knew we were safe. They were artillerymen from a gun emplacement and they took us into their dugout. We stayed there for three days because our squadron was fifty miles away. Eventually, the squadron sent a tender and we were taken back to our airfield. When we got back, I found that all my clothes were packed up in a bundle ready to be sent home. They assumed we'd been killed.

At the end of the war, when the Armistice was announced, everyone heaved a sigh of relief. Then some fool at the aerodrome started a bonfire with some petrol from a can. Everybody got a bit overexcited and people started throwing complete cans of aviation fuel onto the fire. They went up with such a bang that troops nearby thought the war had started again.

They disbanded 11 Squadron at Scopwick in Lincolnshire on the last day of 1919, and I didn't have a job to come back to. It was hard to find any work at all, so I rejoined and went out as a dispatch rider with the Army of Occupation in Germany, based in Cologne. I remember we had a huge Zeppelin shed as a hangar.

When I came back to England and left the air force I bought the bike. I don't know what I paid for it, but it was not a bad bike – a P and M – about 250cc.

I met my late wife Winifred in Cambridge after the war. There were three of us lads in the town at the time and you can imagine what we got up to together. In Cambridge at that time all the students had to wear their caps and gowns. That was one of the rules. Quite often we'd be walking in the town and we'd be stopped by a proctor. He'd say, 'Excuse me, sir, are you a member of the university?' 'No.' 'Thank you very much,' and off he'd go. It was on one of these trips into town that I met Winifred. We married in 1926, and had one daughter, Joy, who also has one daughter. Now we have two great-grandchildren.

After the air force I got work as a draughtsman, and I went to English Electric at Rugby. I was there for some time, until the time came when they couldn't get the orders and if they couldn't get the orders, they didn't want the draughtsmen so we were laid off. They were hard times and I hadn't got any money so I had to go home to my mother and father and I was there for twelve months.

Eventually I got a job as a draughtsman at WH Allen's in Bedford and I was with them for thirty-odd years. I ended up as chief draughtsman and designer. This was a reserved occupation during the Second World War, but I volunteered as an air raid warden and my area was the part of Bedford where we were living. I remember one bomb particularly, because it was dropped over the power station as the planes were flying towards Coventry. They kept bombing Coventry and they had to come over us to get there. We used to do the air warden work when I'd finished work at night.

I used to do night-school teaching as well. I'd go over to St Neots by motorcycle after I'd been at work all day. I did about three evenings a week – one evening I used to have borstal boys for a couple of hours. At first I used to go to the borstal, but then they said if it was better for me, they'd bring the boys to St Neots, so I had them there. I remember once, as I was calling the register, one boy asked to go to the toilet. He never came back so we called the police, who said, 'We know where he's gone.' And they picked him up. On another occasion, as I was writing on the blackboard a strange noise started coming from one boy. 'What's the matter with you?' I asked. 'It's my bird. I love my bird,' he replied. He had a bird in his pocket – I think it had a broken wing, and he was trying to nurse it. You wouldn't have thought a borstal boy would do that.

When I got to a hundred I received the Légion d'honneur from the French in recognition of my service in France over eighty years ago. Then when I got to a hundred and three I was presented with a plaque with the 11 Squadron crest on by two pilots, one who flew in the Second World War and the other was a Tornado pilot from the same squadron which I had flown with before either were born.

Looking back, it's been a good life. A very good life.

John Oborne

4th Battalion, Devonshire Regiment
Born 11 May 1900, *died* 23 October 2004

I was born on 11 May 1900 in Bath and christened in St Saviour's church. I had two sisters, both a lot older than me. I was the little baby of the family; when I was born, they were at a private ladies' school. My father was a butcher and slaughterman. I was about four when I went to a private school where there were children of all ages and we had the one teacher all the time. I was fourteen, nearly fifteen, when I left and I became an apprentice joiner, which wasn't the same as a carpenter. The joiner is the maker and the carpenter is the fixer. We were known as silver ash joiners and I had to buy the tools I needed.

When I was apprenticed, we were on war work. My firm did a lot of naval work, shell boxes and torpedo boxes, that sort of thing. I was working in Bath as that was where the head joiner's shop was but of course we had jobs outside. We worked on the Brecon Council Chambers and the Empire Hotel, which was just about finished when I started work there.

The men from the firm all joined up and went to the war. Most of them went into the Royal Engineers – they could do their bridge building and all such things as that. I joined up at the recruiting place in Bath. I didn't want to go into the Devonshire Regiment – there was no choice, I was just put there. I was fed up with home life, so in the circumstances I was glad to get away. From the age of eleven, there had been a black spot in my life. I've never talked about this, but things were unhappy at home. My mother died when I was fifteen and I lived with my father for a while until he got friendly with the widow next door. My sisters had left home by then, and I also left and never went back again. The army became my home. I still don't make friends all that easily.

The first day of training, we went to Taunton Barracks and were issued with all sorts of different equipment, and the week after that we were shifted to a big camp where we had a straw mattress, a couple of boards, and a couple of little trestles on the floor. From there we were put through the medical – inoculation, vaccination and what have you, and were issued with more equipment. In the third week, we were sent to Cromer, where we trained for five and a half months. We trained on the rifle and Lewis Gun. When we were under bayonet instruction, we used to charge and stick a bayonet into a sack. The sergeant used to bawl at us, 'You couldn't stick the skin off a rice pudding' – along with some other choice words.

It was quite a long training. We were actually brainwashed. I don't think we were worried by news of the casualties at the front. As a matter of fact, I've often thought how our training didn't relate to what we had to face. There was a great deal of red tape – the company drill, physical training, route marches, gymnastics and such things as that, but really and truly the basic training was not really necessary. We used to have company drill on the cliffs near Cromer, and the platoon was a length of string, lined up between two lance corporals and you had to drill between them. It must have been very comical to anyone watching us being string soldiers. You had to do wheeling and turning – and I've thought many times since, 'Why go to all that trouble, when in the end you only had to look after yourself?'

In the training camp we had five companies. When one left for France, another took its place. We were B Company, 4th Battalion. Each platoon had four sections and in each section there was a lance corporal in charge. Then there was a corporal, a sergeant and a second lieutenant – that composed a platoon. We were sent to France in November 1917, we went from Folkestone to Boulogne; there was no crowd to see us off. We had a certain amount of training in France – I forget the name of the place now. We moved on as a company and went into the trenches in 1918.

January and February were fairly quiet. It was good training and you got used to it. We used to sleep anywhere. If you found a place with a bit of a shelter, you slept in it. We would be in the trenches for about six days and then we were brought back to the reserve in Amiens. That was the HQ of the division as far as I know. There were a few older soldiers in the trenches with us. They'd really been through it and told us about it all right. We certainly didn't know of the German push that was about to happen – word of that didn't get to us – but we knew something had to happen one day.

In March we went to Beaumont Hamel. March and April were the worst but about halfway through June the Germans lost their momentum. Then we started to move forward and the Germans

John Oborne, an apprentice before the war, resumed his training as a joiner when he came home, and continued in this trade until he was 75.

called for the Armistice because they didn't want their country overrun by us like they were overrunning other countries. If you notice that, with both wars, as soon as the Allies got near their country, they called for an armistice. They didn't want foreign troops on their ground. You could see it in both wars. As soon as we got near, that was it – we'll have an armistice now.

Lice. I didn't have lice. They had me. The seams of your trousers used to be their nesting place – you'd have to run the seams over a candle. I always remember, there was one chappie, as we were delousing he used to say, 'Ah, little chap. I'm going to put you back – and have you tomorrow when you're bigger.' There was a comical side to it all, but it was dreary sometimes. It's pretty boring, war. It was a hard ten months on the front but we were brainwashed so much that the mind's a blank. I can remember little things, but that's all.

We spent most of the time sat in a hole in the damp old earth. We saw quite a bit of the enemy – as much as they liked to allow us. They weren't idle – they used to do a lot of skirmishing. And we did patrols into no-man's-land, to find out where they were. If we could, we'd bring a prisoner back. We succeeded in that sometimes. It was a very strange war. We saw a lot of the civilians in the villages. They were mostly kind to us – but some weren't. They used to reckon *we* were damaging their country. That was what they blamed *us* for – for damaging their country.

I wouldn't say that there was any one particularly bad moment. Snipers were a problem – they had their pinpoints. The latrines were usually their pinpoint. Not a nice place to die. Those latrines were pretty grim. You'd certainly think so if you'd seen them.

I was lucky in that I was never ill. I was only eighteen and definitely fit as a fiddle. There was entertainment when we were in reserve. We used to watch the concert parties and if we couldn't we'd tell our own dirty stories. I could tell you some of them but I'm not going to. The concert parties weren't bad and some of the men in the cast dressed up as women. Of course they got away with it, you see, it was all right there. You even got the odd evening off. You weren't tied like prisoners.

You never saw the biscuits we had, did you? You know the old-fashioned sort of dog biscuits – square. We used to break them up and try and scrounge some water somewhere and put them in to soak – then open a tin of bully beef and put that in with it. We'd make a bit of a fire and make some soup. You couldn't bite on those biscuits – impossible – they were hard as iron. I had one and cut the middle out of it and put my photograph in it. When I joined up in Cromer, I had a decayed tooth, and I went to see the dentist. The chappie looked at the tooth and I said he might as well pull it out. No, he said, he'd just put some filling in it. 'You're only cannon fodder.' That was what he said. I'd only been in a few weeks and he called me 'cannon fodder'.

In the trenches there were rats with white faces. They often got sick because they got too much meat. Of course you couldn't fire at them and kill them – you couldn't open fire or you'd start the ball rolling again. When it was quiet, you had to stay quiet.

Smells come back to me. You can smell the weather. It's the same now – you can smell the rain, it's a sort of earthy smell. You could smell the snow and the trenches were awful with snow in. If you slipped off the duckboard you were up to your neck. I never did but there was always someone who did. You just had to be careful, but it was all in a day's work. You just did it. Nothing else to do. I never saw anyone do anything spectacular – it was just foot-slogging.

I remember the puttees. You had to put them on pretty tight, or you'd get very wet. I was glad to see that they'd altered that by the Second World War – it was little gaiters instead. That saved a lot of bother, because when you were on parade with puttees, you had to have them just right. But at least we didn't have parades in France.

You had a certain amount of shielding because you used to follow the tanks along. They were a great help. They'd flatten the wire. I know they were in their infancy, but Churchill did a good job with them.

I was never dangerously wounded, but I came pretty close. I was wounded once in the leg but the second time could have been serious. My father gave me a pocket watch when I left for France, which I kept in the left breast pocket of my uniform. My watch was damaged when a bullet hit it. The bullet must have been pretty well spent – as soon as the spin has gone, they're dead. It's the spin that carries them – it's the rifling that spins the bullet. But as soon as the spin has finished it's a dead bullet. Although the watch obviously didn't work again, I kept it as a souvenir. Unfortunately I lost it when I moved homes. We sometimes got buried in mud ourselves – that was a common occurrence. Generally you could still breathe – you just had to help yourself and dig your way out as best you could. It was frightening and if you had to die that way, that was a terrible way to go. Those were the most frightening moments – but it was better than being in an artillery battle.

In those sorts of conditions, in the trenches, the odd person would break down. People were bound to. It was very disturbing. There's no discrimination, you see. You were all in it together – good or bad.

There was no escape and no picking and choosing. A chap who was a bit shaky, he would have appealed for another job in the second war – but there was nothing like that in the first war.

I was earning three shillings a week in my first year's apprenticeship, and me and another apprentice decided to buy a pipe. So we bought a pipe each, and we got some tobacco, and we smoked it. After it was done I wondered, 'What have I gained from that? Nothing.' So that was it. I used to issue cigarettes to the chaps – they could have my share. In the army there was an issue of tobacco and cigarettes. I didn't really like a drink either, but we had rum – and that was a necessity, to keep the wet out, and the cold. And my, did it get cold! It was bitingly cold – it wasn't like a dry cold – it was a damp cold.

At the Armistice I was in a trench, and the Germans opposite got out of theirs, bowed to us and walked off. And that was it. There was nothing to celebrate with – except biscuits.

We stayed after the Armistice and went to Schloßberg. From there you were sent to wherever you had to go. The Allies were in the occupied zone and we were sent to an outpost on the border of no-man's-land. We had duties to police the roads and stop any smuggling of food or other goods across. There was a ten-mile gap between where we were on the wire to the German wire, and it was a rule there that if you saw any of the enemy – or your own men – in the neutral zone, you had to get them back. They were not allowed in the neutral zone, according to the law of war. There were big problems with the local population as well, because a lot of them couldn't go back home. We were a sort of police. One section was on for twenty-four hours and then another took over. We had some casualties during that time – but not too many.

In 1919 we were moving from Wemelskirchen – that was as far as we could go. Burscheid was where all the companies were. I was there from January to the following January. I stayed in the army because I knew I had to buy the tools for my trade when I got home. There was no one to help me. I was a loner. I had no one. I couldn't expect my two sisters to spend any money, let alone the fifty pounds I was going to need for my tools. A saw cost about a pound. When I joined the army, I was on a shilling a day. When we were in France we were given half of that, and the other half was on credit. When I got my stripe, I had an extra sixpence a day. I know I was getting 5/6 a day for a corporal. Not bad. That was nearly £2 a week. So I could have come back home to England in December 1918 but I thought things out and I left the army at the start of 1920. They held on to your money and paid you what had accrued when you left. The quartermasters did very well out of it – you didn't know what they were up to.

Back in England, I just had one of my sisters living in Bath, and I went to stay with her and I carried on where I'd left off. I went and saw the secretary of my old company about resuming my apprenticeship. He said, 'Well, sonny, you know the wages now for apprentices are far different from when you went away. A fourth-year apprentice gets a pound a week. And in the fifth year you get twenty-five shillings a week.' I had less than I was earning in the army. I had to do it though – the army wasn't my career. I finished my apprenticeship. After that, if you were showing signs of being a good workman, you were put out as an improver. You had two thirds of a joiner's money. A joiner then was earning 1/6 an hour, so I got a shilling an hour.

I stayed with the firm until I was seventy-five. I wasn't with them all the time but I was attached to them, on their payroll. They gave me £500 when I left. They had a job to do that – it's not a pensionable job, you see.

I did some private work on boats. One of the clients was a Frenchman with a yacht – *The Wanderer*. I was the only one he'd have to work on it – he wouldn't have anyone else. One day I was doing some library shelves at Denbigh, when the Frenchman said he had a little job that needed doing down on *The Wanderer*. The firm sent another chappie down; the Frenchman arrived and saw this other lad using his level. Well – you can't use a level in a boat and the Frenchman said, 'Put those tools back in your bag. I'll wait for Jack to come back.' The Frenchman was very good to me – he wouldn't have no one else.

The Wanderer went down at Dunkirk. That was the end of it. I had spent years on her.

In 1938 I voluntarily joined the Civil Defence. I was living in Bath and I became an ARP warden. But I never thought after what we had been through that we would ever go to war again. When Germany started using V1 flying bombs, doodlebugs as most people called them, London and south-east England became a target. As this became a war zone the Civil Defence Services became stretched and needed help. I volunteered my services and was sent to Surrey, around Coulsdon and Purley – the area between Croydon up to London was known as 'doodlebug alley'. Although the doodlebugs were aimed at London, if their fuel cut off early, then that was the area they landed. The effect could be devastating. If a bomb had dropped we'd go and see who we could rescue – then get the place a bit ship-shape.

I shall never forget one time there was a woman with a library down at Brighton, which they'd moved up to this house in Purley. A flying bomb pitched into the grounds in front of the house. And this woman was stood in her front room surrounded by the wreckage – thousands of books all round her – absolutely dazed. I always remember that – she was utterly bewildered. She didn't know where she was. But to move from Brighton up there was asking for trouble. The rescue people would pull people out of the wreckage. Our duty was to see that the lights were out and such things as that. Those flying bombs, they'd go up and pitch down, but they didn't dig a shell hole. They caused a surface explosion and shattered the surrounding area in that way.

I married Evelyn Constance Cooper in 1925. I met her when I was in the army and she was 'commandeered'. In those days, the Labour Exchange would have you registered and they'd send you to different parts. Her home was in Chippenham at first. I never pursued the courtship when I came out of the army – it was just an accidental meeting some time later. She died in March 1985 – if she'd have lived 'til June, we would have been married sixty years. We had a son, David, and now I have a grandson and four great-grand-children.

I've had a happy life. Oh yes – I enjoyed it. What would I say now to an eighteen-year-old boy? I suppose I'd say, 'At work, make a good job of it and be more polite to people – have better manners.' A lot of them haven't today. I don't think they'll ever be wanted for a war – but if they were, they haven't got the stamina. They couldn't stand what we went through in the First World War. The youth of today couldn't stand it.

My son, who has sat with us today, has learned a great deal about me that he didn't know – I know he has. It seems I've kept it all to myself. I didn't want to worry anyone. I've managed to pull through, and I did it off my own bat. I got no parental help. Would my father have been proud of me? No, I don't think so. It didn't seem as though he worried over us at all. He might have cared – but I never knew. But my mother would have been proud; I was the apple of her eye. I don't say I miss her now – I'm very philosophical about it. I've no idea what the secret is to living so long. I just keep on – a bit like an infantryman.

Kenneth Cummins

Royal Naval Reserve · *Born* 6 March 1900

I was born in Richmond in Surrey – and I had two brothers and a sister. I was the eldest. They're all gone now. My father was in the Merchant Navy.

I went to the Merchant Taylors' School in Liverpool – in fact it was in Crosby, between Liverpool and Southport. I remember going to Blundell Sands nearby to watch Graham White flying in his single-engine biplane. The plane was attached by rope to a large stake in the sand. He'd start it up and when it had worked up enough power we boys, who'd be in charge of the rope, would release it – and he'd take off. You've heard the expression 'Pigs might fly'? Well on one occasion, Graham White took a live pig up with him and flew it over Liverpool.

I trained with the OTC at school – and I was on manoeuvres, training with the King's Liverpool Rifles, when war was declared. We used to march behind them, with a band playing. That was the only training I had.

Kenneth Cummins, right, in naval cadet uniform, was already in the school's Officer Training Corps when the war began. Age fifteen, he left school to join HMS *Worcester*, moored on the Thames, for training before going to sea.

I was fourteen at the outbreak of war and Liverpool was an exciting city to be in. At the school you didn't have to leave at fifteen – it was voluntary. But at eighteen, there were boys leaving school to go into the army and go to the Western Front. Masters left for the army too – and some came back again to teach – minus an arm or a leg. Some were very fierce and would beat us.

When I was fifteen I applied to P&O, hoping I could get one of their scholarships as a naval cadet. There didn't seem much chance, as hundreds applied – but then fifty of us were invited to a grand dinner with liveried servants and masses of silverware. Perhaps they were looking to see who knew the right knives and forks to use. Anyway, I was accepted, and I went to HMS *Worcester*. I was there two years, which was the minimum. We were on the Thames there, and we all had jolly boats – it was a good time.

I was not addressed as midshipman at this stage – I was a cadet. The training was a mixture of seamanship and skilled work. You had to have a certificate when you left. I can't remember if it was December 1917 or January 1918 when I left. I was nearly eighteen. Discipline was very strict on the *Worcester* – it was to get us in trim. If we failed to do something correctly, for instance, we'd have to stand for hours holding a bucket of water over our heads. In 1917, I was on the *Worcester* when I saw a raid by a Zeppelin – we were based on the Thames, near Gravesend. The Zeppelin was shot down in flames.

I remember the flu epidemic very well. While I was at school I remember going down to the pier head in Liverpool where we saw corpses being carried off US troopships of men who had died from flu.

When I left the *Worcester*, I joined HMS *Morea*. By this time I was a midshipman RNR. We'd been on a land-based ship, and our first going to sea was on the *Morea*, from England to Freetown in Sierra Leone. The *Morea* was an armed cruiser and we escorted ships transporting troops. We protected the Atlantic convoys. I spent something like six months ferrying the troops between the two places. We never crossed all the way to the States – the troops went to Freetown and they were escorted on to Cape Town by another cruiser. They were going to East Africa, I imagine.

I was very shocked on my first voyage out. In June 1918 we were in the Bristol Channel, quite well out to sea, and suddenly we began going through corpses. The Germans had sunk a British hospital ship, the *Llandover Castle*, and we were sailing through floating bodies. We were not allowed to stop – we just had to go straight through. It was quite horrific, and my reaction was to vomit over the edge. It was something we could never have imagined . . . particularly the nurses: seeing these bodies of women and nurses, floating in the ocean, having been there some time. Huge aprons and skirts in billows, which looked almost like sails because they'd dried in the hot sun. There was no chance of rescuing them – they were all dead. As a fighting ship – which we were – we were not permitted to stop unless ordered to do so by the admiral.

I didn't do very many voyages, because the war came to an end. We never had to open fire – but we were well armed with six-inch guns and more. In those days you'd get six-inch guns on merchant ships too – at the stern. A merchant ship is not allowed by law to have the guns anywhere else but in the stern. They were purely for defence – anything else would be offensive. However, we were a naval ship, flying the White Ensign, and I had a gun allocated to me – every midshipman had a gun – and there was a lieutenant in charge. While we were at sea there were a few alarms – but we never got shot at or attacked by submarines. At eighteen you don't have any responsibility and can take things lightly.

I was a midshipman – the most junior officer in the navy. I carried a dirk – that was your arms as a midshipman. I was in uniform from the age of fifteen – as soon as I joined the *Worcester*. After the training I got a midshipman's badge and never wore civilian clothes again until after I left the *Worcester*.

When the war ended I don't think I had any particular feelings but I wasn't numb. None of my family died in the war – I was the only one who was in it.

Five weeks before the end of the war, the *Otranto* went down after a collision with another ship off the island of Islay. One of my good friends was thought to be lost, but while I was down in Devonport, I saw him walking towards me. I said, 'My God, you must be a ghost!' You had a different aspect on death during the war. So many were killed on the *Otranto* – when the *Kashmir* ran her down, she sank, and of course the personnel were drowned.

When I was fourteen, at the very beginning of the war, I remember hearing about the loss of the *Aboukir*. About ninety midshipmen were killed – sunk by a U-boat. *Cressy* and *Hogue* went to rescue them and the same submarine hit them both with torpedoes – the U-boat sank all three.

After the First World War I left the Royal Navy and joined the Merchant Navy with P&O. This was by arrangement, as they had paid half of my cadet fees. I joined them as a cadet in 1919, and I was qualified as an officer in 1921. Immediately after the war we made some trips transporting Australian troops home – they were exuberant and very lively – full of life. They were so pleased to be going home after the fighting, it was only natural. When we arrived at Sydney on one trip, there had been flu on board, so the troops were made to stay in quarantine but they were so desperate to go home that they all jumped overboard. Sydney Harbour was full of sharks, but they didn't care.

Between the wars, as an officer on a P&O liner, I was on the bridge – so I didn't have anything to do with the passengers – nothing at all, apart from saying hello. I was on the bridge all the time. Whilst I was on the *Macedonia* in about 1923, we brought Lord Carnarvon's body back from Egypt in a coffin that weighed five tons. He was the man who had financed the search for Tutankhamun's tomb and who died weeks after it was discovered. He died of a mosquito bite, although he was supposed to have been a victim of 'The Curse of the Pharaohs'. Another time we transported an Indian prince who actually died on board. His body had to be preserved as there was going to be a special burial ceremony in India and the ship's doctor solved this problem by putting the body in an ice-box bath.

At the outbreak of the Second World War, the P&O ships were commandeered as troop carriers. I remained as chief officer on the converted liner, the *Viceroy of India*. She was very well equipped and luxurious. She was turbo-electric, so there was no vibration – she was my favourite of all the ships I sailed on, but sadly she was sunk on 11 November 1942. We were returning from transporting troops of the North African invasion force to Algiers and were travelling back empty, about forty miles off the North African coast. It was around half past four in the morning, while I was having my coffee. I had just arrived on the bridge. There was the most enormous bang and an explosion in the engine room. We'd been hit by a submarine – she'd probably been on the surface, recharging her batteries and had seen or heard us.

Chief Officer Cummins (front row centre) on P&O ship
Viceroy of India, on cruise to the North Cape before
the Second World War.

The armed troopship *Viceroy of India* sinks after
landing 2000 troops at Oran as part of the Allied
North African invasion force, 11 November 1942.

The engine room is the worst place to be hit – she never moved again – and because it was right in the middle of the bulkhead, we started taking on water. It took four hours to sink, which was quite long enough to get into life boats, and there were no troops aboard. It's an irony because I have a photograph of all the ships which carried the troops for the North African landing as they went past Gibraltar. The Germans must have been furious when they realised that they had allowed this huge armada of ships to pass safely – and they sank our ship which was empty with only a skeleton crew.

We lost four of our crew – all were in the engine room. You couldn't help anyone there – if they didn't die at once, they drowned later. As chief officer, I was sent down to check how long the ship could stay afloat – all I had was a little flashlight. The water was pouring in and the noise of it coming through was horrendous. I still have dreams about it.

It was a nice calm day – and at seven o'clock the captain gave the order to abandon ship. There was no panic – everyone knew the drill and everybody had a job to do. Some sailors came on deck with suitcases, but they had to leave them. As chief officer I went to my cabin and put on my best uniform, but I left all my personal belongings behind. It was a shame – the maharajahs used to give rather striking presents to officers on ships that carried them back to India. We climbed on board the lifeboats and watched the ship go down at around eight o'clock. It was a very unpleasant sight. We were picked up later by HMS *Boudicca*. That was my only sinking.

I became chief officer on the *Ile de France* – which had been a crack ship of the French fleet. It had been at Singapore when the British found it after the fall of France and commandeered it – and I spent nine months in New York overseeing her conversion to a troopship. Then we made regular voyages carrying troops only. There were five large ships crossing the Atlantic with troops and we were one, carrying around 10,000 men at a time – and then there was the *Queen Mary*, the *Queen Elizabeth*, each carrying 15,000, and the *Mauretania*. We sailed alone, but we were capable of 25 knots, so there wasn't much danger, as this was faster than any German submarine.

In 1945 I went to the *Maloja* as chief officer, and eventually took over as captain – it was my first command. We were sailing to the African coast, taking Italian prisoners of war back home, and Zulus back to Africa. I wasn't impressed with the Italians' discipline but the Zulus were a fine class of men – cheerful and well disciplined. They were returning to their own country after time away. The consequences of the war went on for a couple of years afterwards – ships were returning to their duties, and they all required overhauling.

I was with P&O a further thirteen years after 1947, serving on various ships. These were the great years of the Merchant Navy – it didn't flourish after about 1960. I would not have liked to have been at sea over the last forty years or so. It's another world now. In many ways I feel the Merchant Navy was never recognised for the huge contribution we made in carrying troops and armaments to and fro. The Royal Navy kept England free of intruders and played its part in the fighting, and the Merchant Navy played their part in bringing food and fuel to the country. Between them, equally in my opinion, we kept the country going in wartime.

When I was fifty-two I met my wife, Rosemary, on a voyage from Australia – she was on a visit to England. We married in Sydney. We had four children, two boys and two girls. One daughter is a barrister and the other is married with children, one son is an accountant

Chief Officer Cummins on left – aboard *Ile de France* – in 1944.

and the other son is in hospital management. I always encouraged my children to do what they wanted in life and of course I'm proud of my daughter, but I think in general women should look after the children and run the home and men should work and support them. Call me old-fashioned if you like.

Since the First World War, England has not prospered. We have lost an empire and suffered because of this. Overall I find it hard to think of any advances.

The world was a quiet and pleasant place when I was young. There is too much noise today and I don't approve of it. Of course there *have* been advances made, but not all improvements are for the better. We can now travel supersonic but what's the use of that? We can get to the moon or Mars. So what? We had candles in my day, not electric light. There was nothing wrong with that. You just went to bed earlier. The Church of England has certainly deteriorated. Now we have women priests and all sorts – and the Church can't even manage its own finances. My outlook is old-fashioned – my sons tell me that all the time.

I'm not convinced about medical advancements either. Certainly, modern hygiene is better, but nowadays you have people being kept alive when they are cabbages. Is that any better for them or for us? In my day, they died off.

On the other hand, I would say that I had some wonderful work done on my eyes a few years back. I lost my sight completely for three months, but now I have the sight back in one eye and I can read my newspaper every morning. I never thought I'd be able to do that again.

What has kept me going? I had a good diet all my life, being on board ship, and I always drank in moderation – never had the chance to do anything else. I smoked a pipe from a very young age. I started to put on weight when I became captain, but it was not from dining with the passengers. We may have carried some famous people – film stars and so on – but I wouldn't have been interested. We once carried King Farouk, but no British royals – and we once carried Lady Clementine Churchill, on the *Stratheden*. And the other thing is discipline – my own and other people's. I respect discipline and there's a lack of it today.

But mostly I think love has been the most important thing. Not sex, although sex is part of love. Love brings contentment, which brings good health. Misery and unhappiness leads to ill health. It's not just the love of a husband or wife, but of one's children and family.

Nicholas Swarbrick

Merchant Navy · *Born* 14 November 1898, *died* 2 February 2006

I was born on 14 November 1898 in Grimsargh and that's where I am now. Outside the window of this room here is a field, and my father, who had quite a number of interests including farming, used to farm the land just outside this window when I was a boy. He rented it from the then occupier of Grimsargh House. His land extended roughly as far as the railway station. I played in these fields a hundred years ago so I have come full circle. I have been round the world but I have come to rest where I was born.

My father was a Roman Catholic. In his early days, he went to Usher College in Durham, originally with the idea of becoming a priest. Usher College was a seminary for training priests and he had four years there in the late 1800s. I think he met my mother very much later when he would have been about twenty-nine. Mother died quite early of tuberculosis. In those days tuberculosis was incurable, and it was rampant. I was about four when Mother died, so I never really had a mother. I had one sister and a brother, and my sister died of the same disease as our mother – consumption again. She was in her late teens or early twenties. My brother was two years younger than I was, so he was just two when Mother died – he was just a baby. Of course, in those days, consumption used to establish itself, then it became infectious, but it was not infectious in the early stages. It became infectious in my mother when I was about two, and for that reason we had to be kept away from her, which of course for a mother was a dreadful situation. I can remember having to keep some distance away on account of her coughing. So I never had a mother in the ordinary sense of the word – the sort of mother where you could fly into her arms. That was the last thing I was allowed to do. Usually a youngster flies into his mother's arms, doesn't he? That was the very thing I was banned from doing. I didn't know any different, though. My sister was seven years older than I was, so she was in a position on mother's death to run the household. She had had a convent education in Preston at Larkhill, where there was a Catholic church – St Ignatius, I think it was. It was run by nuns, and the fact that they had a church next door was almost essential to their existence. She looked after me – with varying degrees of success.

My first school was Alston Hall – in the next parish to Grimsargh, which was one of the Alston and Dilworth parishes of the district of Longridge. My father was chairman of the Longridge Urban District Council for fifty years. What he didn't know about the drains and sewers in the district wasn't worth knowing.

I suppose I was about four when I went to primary school. I did that until I could read and write, and then I was sent to the Catholic college in Winkley Square, Preston for secondary education when I was about six. I walked to the primary school but I took the train to

Nicholas Swarbrick, a keen student of radio technology, was quickly promoted to Radio Operator on joining the Merchant Navy, and served on trans-Atlantic routes transporting troops.

the Catholic college. My house was next door to the railway, and you could wait until the train was actually in the station and then run out to catch it. It was a steam train in those days – it was a journey of about twenty minutes to the station at Ribbleton, then Deepdale – a more important station, then you went under a tunnel, and out at Maudland, which was adjoining the main line which runs on that side of Preston. We more or less behaved ourselves on the train, but we had some high jinks. I'd put my head out of the window of the train, which you lowered on a leather strap and the ash from the smokestack would blow into my eyes.

I was not very keen on games, I'd much rather read a book. We played marbles, of course, and conkers. There was a splendid chestnut tree very close at hand and I remember throwing stones at the tree to dislodge them.

Our house was four up and four down and I shared a large bedroom with my father but there was lots of room. When I left school, it was one of the tragedies in my life. The Jesuits ran Stoney-hurst College and the Catholic college for boys in Winkley Square Preston was staffed by the same Jesuits as the college. These Jesuits were very much inclined to use what they called the leather strap – a farrular – like the devil. In my first two or three forms at the college I did very well academically. Each week we had a card which we took to our parents. It had four designations on it – the first was excellent, the next good, the next fair, and poor. In the first three forms I always had 'excellent' – excellent on conduct and applica-tion. And I always got sixpence from my father for that.

The college had two separate buildings, the juniors in one building and the seniors in the other. When I moved into the senior building there was one particular Jesuit priest. We'd had one in the other building, but he was marvellous and I adored him and most of us pupils did jolly well under him. But when we moved to the next college, we got a chap called Father Ellison, and he was a devil with the farrular. And this was a major tragedy in my life. On one particular occasion I had a lot of homework, and I was given a lot of irregular verbs – horrible things. To be honest, I did my best, but Father Ellison hit me so hard and hurt me so badly that I refused to go back to school. My father more or less acquiesced, and my education was ruined. Although I was instinctively a studious person, that ruined my education. Nowadays, Father Ellison would have been jailed for what he did to us. I know the Jesuits had a national reputation for caning knowledge into pupils, but it's an absolute anathema today. I was born fifty years too soon – what has happened in the last fifty years has been more far-reaching than in all the previous centuries together. That really is true. The last fifty years have made such a difference to the world as a whole, and the revolution is going on. Strictly speaking, if I'd had my way, I would have gone to the Church of England grammar school where there was no farrular, but religious intolerance was fairly rampant, and I wouldn't have been allowed. I continued my studies privately. I read very extensively – not fiction but non-fiction. I read anything, so that I am a self-educated man. After that incident I stayed at home and no one came in to teach me. I only wish they had. I was fourteenish when I left school.

I was interested in my father's business affairs and I helped him for a year or two but the war was looming. Although farming was my father's chief joy, he didn't spend most of his time on it. He was very much in the public eye in Longridge and did a great deal of public work. As a young man, I was very interested in all things electrical and scientific things generally, but in those days radio was unknown to the average person.

I do remember the funeral of Edward VII in 1910, and I remember the coronation of George V. I remember that the children nationally were given a cup or mug. I was born in Queen Victoria's reign, then came Edward VII – I lived through two changes of reign and got two cups. I read about George V's coronation in the newspaper. I also remember the sinking of the *Titanic* – this is coming very close to home. On my second ship in the war, we watched a silent film, which made a big impression on me. One of the survivors gave an account of racing up the main stairs in the centre of the ship as the water was rising up the stairs. He had to run to race the water and he got out and was one of those who survived. I remember the agony of the account. I remember him talking about the ship sinking by the bow. She hit the iceberg in the bow, and one of the funnels was held in position by stays but they were never designed to have this angle on them, and one of the funnels crashed down on to the deck below. The stays could no longer hold it – there was a terrific rumpus when that happened – which added to the turmoil. Later, during the war, when I was bringing American troops across from New York to Liverpool, we passed over the site of the wreck of the *Titanic* – we knew we were passing over it. As a radio operator, I was in communication later on with the Cape Race, which was the station that the *Titanic* communicated with in Newfoundland – and that was only five years later.

When the Great War started I was working with my father – I was very interested in radio, although most people didn't know what it was. I took a course in Liverpool learning Morse code and mastering the technique of using the instruments. Many of the ships had been running without radio and because of the U-boat menace they were desperately in need of radio operators. I got my certificate of proficiency, and within four or five days I was sailing out of London and through the Straits of Dover right into the thick of it. The radio operating on the ship I was rushed into was German, but it was a British ship. Most of the British ships had a contract with Marconi, but this particular one had a contract with a German firm. The ship was the *Westfalia* – it was owned in Glasgow by a firm called Gow Harrison. They gave me a uniform and made me a merchant naval officer. I had no duties except the radio. We had to keep continuous watch, and what with relieving each other for meals, we did a fourteen-hour day all told. Then we crossed to Canada, bringing loads of horses from the Atlantic coast – from Halifax. We did several voyages from Halifax and later on from Montreal. Our main cargo was horses – no troops.

I'm not quite sure how many torpedoes missed us but ships were being sunk all around me. I was in the unenviable position of knowing before anyone else what was going on, on account of the radio and the distress calls. I was very much aware of the danger I was sharing with the people who were already being torpedoed. We picked up Morse from the other ships – that was the essence of my job – either from another ship or from shore. I could pick up an SOS from a ship in our convoy that was under attack but we never stopped to pick up survivors because if you did you'd be torpedoed. You'd be a sitting duck for the sub. I knew that people were being left to die – but this was war.

When I was on the Atlantic route bringing American troops over, I remember there were three stations that spanned the Atlantic – one was the Eiffel Tower which was magnificently high. The second was Arlington in America, and the third was Poldhu, in Cornwall. Those were the three stations that we could hear all through. We were not allowed, nor were we able to communicate with them – we could only receive. Our transmissions were not capable of crossing continents. I remember the tonal quality of the transmissions from Poldhu. They came through at a sedate pace, in a low pitch that made it easy to recognise the call letters. It was at Poldhu that Marconi had first transmitted the letter 'S' across the Atlantic and demonstrated the potential of wireless radio. The other transmitters had their own individual nuances. The French transmitter sounded like a bleating sheep.

When the big explosion happened at Halifax, in December 1917, I was very fortunate in not being there at the time, because we had loaded our horses at the very same berth a few days earlier. We had embarked the horses there. There was a terrific explosion – it wrecked the port. A German submarine blew up a ship carrying ammunition for France. It was a dreadful calamity. It put Halifax out of action for a long time, and the port was very much needed for getting stuff to France from Canada. I can't remember if we were at sea when we heard about it. Messages were few and far between – there was a clampdown. They didn't want the Germans to know the extent of the damage, but really they jolly well knew.

Travel in those days was by sea only. Eventually I set foot on every continent except for South America. It's an awful long voyage, for instance, coming from Melbourne to Liverpool in a 13-knotter cargo boat. Mind you, we had a roundabout itinerary, leaving Melbourne and going up the east coast to Brisbane, then Townsville. At Townsville we loaded. The ship I was on was equipped to carry horses. What most people don't realise is that, in the First World

War, everything that moved had a horse attached. There were a few staff cars, but for the most part the war was conducted on the backs of horses. I hadn't even seen a motor car until around 1908, though my godfather was one of the first persons to buy a motor car – it was a French one, actually. This would be about 1904 or 5 – motor cars were very, very scarce in those days. I remember if you saw a motor car as boys in those days, we crowded around as if it was something out of a dream.

When the Armistice was announced in November 1918, we were on our way back to the UK. In the last six or seven months of the war we were bringing American troops over from New York to Liverpool on an Atlantic liner owned by Canadian Pacific Railways. Before the war, Canadian Pacific decided to go maritime, and instead of starting rival ships to the ones that were running, they bought up the existing ships – it was a masterstroke. The Germans, before the actual Armistice, were already in retreat. On our last voyage we were getting the news from Eiffel Tower regarding the Germans. The news was very brief, but they said that the Germans continue to withdraw on all fronts. We published a newspaper on board and I remember day after day that that was all I could tell them. But it was enough.

It was quite a dark and secret world in radio. We had a code book, and we had this in the radio room – we were the only persons with the time and the knowledge to use it. It was all in five-letter code, and very tedious indeed. On the liner there were two of us – we were completely detached from the running of the ship. We were running our own department and we were not interfered with – nor did we interfere with the ship. We were engrossed in our own world. We tried to mind our own business. When messages came through, we had no typewriter – so we hand-wrote the messages in fountain pen and then communicated by blow-pipe to the bridge. They were able to communicate with us and vice versa when the need arose. Under war conditions, we couldn't use a messenger because by the time he'd delivered his message, we might have been torpedoed. It had to be instant.

There was very little entertainment on board – it was, after all, war conditions. After the war it was quite a different thing. I was very fortunate to be posted to the Yeoward Line of Liverpool – they had banana groves in the Canary Islands and they had three ships – banana boats – which carried about ninety paying passengers. From my point of view, I had no duties in port, so that in Brisbane and Madeira and in the Canaries we were free to join the passengers in their pursuits. After a while we got to know the places, so the passengers were delighted to have a free guide, and we were equally delighted to have quite a lot of young ladies. From a young man's point of view it was heaven on earth. Once, I believe, I almost fell in love!

I was in the Merchant Navy through the twenties – the perfect time to be at sea. I know Portugal very well indeed, and we had four days every three weeks and a day or two in Lisbon, and a day in Madeira, and two or three days in Las Palmas and Tenerife. As you can imagine, I thoroughly enjoyed that. I still came out of it a bachelor.

I left the Merchant Navy after the Great Crash. I was in the Trossachs in Scotland while the ship was in Grangemouth. I had a cycle on board, and I cycled from Grangemouth into the Trossachs, and while I was there, I heard the news. The pound and the dollar – the whole financial establishment – was on the verge of collapse. I was so appalled by the circumstances that I decided there and then to come home. My father had a lot of investments in government stocks and these were falling like anything. I persuaded him that he had to get out of government stocks – and into property. In order to do that, I gave up my sea career and came home to help him run the property he bought.

He bought several farms, and I remember the bank manager saying to him, 'You know, Mr Swarbrick, you're buying yourself a whole lot of trouble.' The bank manager was right – and I came to deal with the trouble. My father died in March 1947, and after that I took on several farms and started farming myself. I remember going over one of the big farms – a 200-acre farm – with a prospective tenant, and right in the middle of this visit, I thought, 'Damn it all! What on earth am I doing? I want to farm this land myself!' So I did. I took a great deal of interest later on in how to breed better cattle, and was very fortunate in meeting a Cambridge University professor who was very keen on eugenics and on cattle improvement. He and I and several other people formed the Breeders' Study Group, and we used to gather together in Cambridge for the first three days of every New Year to hear the professor lecture on cattle improvement.

I never married. On the whole I regard myself as lucky to have escaped, because no sooner has she knobbled you, than her interest changes. She's no longer interested in you but in children. It's true, you know. And you're just an adjunct.

Ted Rayns

Army Service Corps · *Born* 9 February 1899, *died* 30 December 2004

I was born on 9 of February 1899 in Manchester. I had four sisters and three brothers. My father was in the fire brigade. I went to a primary school and when I passed my exams at eleven, I went on to the high school. I left when I was fourteen. I used to walk to school dressed in a smock and a cap that my father bought me. It wasn't too far to walk. I was the oldest of the brothers, so I used to walk on my own.

I remember going with my dad to watch Newton Heath play football. They became Manchester United in 1902 but I saw them when they were still called Newton Heath. I remember how vast the stand was, with all its steps. There was no tea at half-time, but we did have pies.

When I left school, I went into a factory. One day I had an accident in the factory. I didn't know if they would take me back after that so I decided to join the army instead. When I told my father what I intended to do, he told me that it was the best thing I could have done.

Ted Rayns, pictured here with his sisters.

I joined the Army Service Corps. I trained in Bradford, where they taught us to drive. It was all mechanical. We didn't learn to ride horses. After training was finished, we were sent to France. I was acting sergeant. When we arrived at Rouen, we lined up our ambulances and started filling them up with petrol. Unfortunately, one of the saps was smoking, and we ended up losing four ambulances. We had to push them into the sand. That was my experience of being a sergeant. Soon after that, I changed from acting sergeant to a dispatch rider – riding a Douglas 350.

As a dispatch rider, I never carried a rifle or a revolver. I was on the Somme, relaying orders and instructions to gun batteries. Whenever I went up, I watched the batteries firing away. When I first arrived, the batteries were using homing pigeons to carry messages but the Germans kept shooting them down and after a while field telephones began to be used. I was usually carrying my messages to the officers' wooden huts.

At the Armistice, I was on the St Omer road. I had Spanish flu. I was sent to a hospital that normally treated people with venereal disease. They cleared the hospital out and began using it for victims of the flu – Germans as well. It was terrible. I had a temperature and I had all sorts of injections. I had it for more than three weeks. It wasn't just soldiers who were infected – civilians had it too.

We ate Maconochie's bully beef throughout the war – we never got any real meat. Even in reserve, away from the front, it was bully beef. The Chinese used to cook it.

After the Armistice I stayed with a family in Cologne, whilst serving with the Army of Occupation. After that, I was sent down the Rhine to Holland. From there I was discharged.

During the war, one of my brothers, who was in the army, died after being kicked by a horse. Another brother was in the fire service.

When I came back I took a job in a car and body fitting company in Nottingham. I was a mechanic, working on trailers. I met my first wife, Beatrice, in Birmingham. We had two children and we moved to Leicester, where I ran a shop. During the Second World War I was in the fire service. My father wrote a letter recommending me to them. I remember fighting one particularly big fire in Cornwall. Beatrice died when she was sixty-one and a couple of years later I married Hilda, my second wife.

I've never tasted alcohol in my life. I took an oath with the Quakers to remain a teetotaller. Nor have I ever smoked. I eat well – fish and chips, anything really, but I don't eat a lot of pork. I was ill for a while recently but I recovered and came out of hospital. I've had a happy life. Things still worry me but I've never spoken much about my wartime experiences. Nowadays, it's hard to remember. It was all such a long time ago.

William Elder

Royal Garrison Artillery · *Born* 5 May 1897, *died* 22 June 2005

I was born in 1897 on 5 May, in Selkirk. I was the eldest – I had a sister, Isabella, who was two years younger than me, and a brother James, born ten years after me.

I grew up in Selkirk on the Philiphaugh Estate – that was where my father worked as groom – and I went to school at the Philiphaugh School. I remember one teacher there particularly well – he was my Uncle Walter. We called him 'Foosey Beard' because he had such a long beard. The school was two miles away, and we walked there and back each day.

I can remember the first car in our area. It belonged to a man called Billy Strang Steel. The man who had been his coachman became his chauffeur – but he was only used to horses. He hadn't got the hang of steering and braking, so the car ended up in a field off the Yarrow Road. We had games after school. We'd play cricket in summer – and in winter there were board games at home – but our father would tip the board over if we argued among the three of us.

We used to go with our friends to the 'Happy Hunting Grounds' where the Ettrick and Yarrow rivers meet. We went for walks with our aunts and uncles up Harehead Hill, often past coops of young pheasants with their broody hens.

When I left school I got an apprenticeship as a gardener on the Bowhill Estate. That lasted three years, and I started on eight shillings a week for the first year. It went up to ten bob the second year, then twelve shillings for the last year.

In Yarrow I remember Mary Whillans married one of the two Wilson brothers from the Middle Lodge. She had a hard time keeping them in order. At one bad stage, the single brother asked her, 'What do you think WE married you for?'

When I was about eighteen, my family moved to Mount Melville, and I was going to go on training – but by then it was 1915, and they wanted people to join up and fight in France. So I joined up under the Derby Scheme. I went to the Royal Garrison Artillery – as a gunner – and soon we were sent to France.

I was there at some of the big battles. The Somme, and the second battle for Ypres. I lost many friends – it was a terrible time and conditions were dreadful, but I had my duties to do, looking after the horses. We had horses to draw the guns and they needed to be cared for. I was the team master and that was what I did. Those horses were loyal friends to us and many died alongside us.

Towards the end of the war, I came home on leave once and I got the train as far as Duns, then I had to walk a good long way carrying this heavy kitbag. When I got home I found they'd all gone down with flu – everyone was in bed.

When I got back from France after the war I went back to my

William Elder, age sixteen. At this time he had left school and had started as an apprentice gardener on the nearby Bowhill Estate with a wage of eight shillings a week.

job gardening. I got work on the estate of the Duke of Buccleuch and that's where I met my wife, Daisy Otter.

Later on I worked tending cemeteries in Selkirk and Kirkcaldy. Many of them had graves for the boys who were lost in France – some of them were friends of mine.

When we married we lived in Selkirk, while my parents were at Drygrange. If we wanted to visit them we had to go by pony and trap. The whole family set off one day on a visit – Daisy and me and the two bairns, Kathleen and Tom – and on the way back the pony just stopped outside a shop and wouldn't budge. We had to finish the journey on foot. That same pony used sometimes to jump the fence out of the field if it got startled by the local hunt going through. One time it jumped and got stuck, half in and half out of the paddock. The huntsmen had to stop and lift it off.

In 1938 we moved to Kirkcaldy in Fife. When the Second World War began, I was forty-two, so I joined the LDV – the Home Guard – and my son Tom went into the Black Watch. I joined the British Legion and the Kirkcaldy United Services Institute. We greatly increased the Poppy Day collection and as Secretary of the KUSI I spent many hours writing to the Earl Haig Fund, helping to get pensions for returning servicemen for their war service and for war widows. After the war we moved to work at Hayfield Cemetery, and we stayed there until I retired. All the time I loved my own garden, growing vegetables and fruit – and I used to keep bees too. Some say that bees give people who keep them the gift of long life.

In 1963 Daisy and I visited my sister Ella out in New Zealand, and I did some part-time work there at a sheep-farmers' store – but we came back and retired to Kettering – that was where our Kathleen and her family were. Then in 1978 Daisy died, and later, after

William Elder found that his duties caring for the horses which drew the heavy guns kept him focused as he saw many of his friends killed and injured around him.

Kathleen's husband died, she and I travelled back to the borders – to our roots. That trip was when I was ninty-nine.

One day my granddaughter Dawn came home from school – she had been learning about Ypres. She was telling me all about it – and I simply said, 'I know, dear. I was there.'

George Hardy

5th Inniskilling Dragoons
Born 2 December 1899, *died* 22 January 2005

I was born in Kingston-upon-Hull, and my parents were Henry and Alice Hardy. My father was a merchant seaman and was away from home a great deal, so I spent a lot of time helping my mother when I was young. She ran a small corner shop from our home and baked bread every night, and I'd sell this on the streets nearby before going to school.

I joined the army in 1917 – the 5th Inniskilling Dragoons, which was the cavalry, even though I'd never sat on a horse before. I was only seventeen at the time, so I lied about my age to get in.

The forces were all different in those days. The cavalry regiments aren't around now – at least, not with horses – they have tanks now. But I did my training in the desert, with not a single house or building for a hundred miles around.

I remember we used to sing a lot of Irish songs in the Inniskillings, being an Irish regiment. Captain Oates, who went with Scott on his expedition to reach the South Pole and had been in the regiment, was a hero of ours.

George Hardy in uniform of 5th Inniskilling Dragoons in 1918.

We were just about to set out for France in 1918 when the Armistice was declared while my unit was preparing for combat, so I didn't see any action. By then I was a cavalry instructor. The most action I saw was in the army rugby team, playing against a New Zealand army team. I was on the field for just a few minutes – I got pummelled and had to be taken off.

After the war we went to Egypt, and it was while we were there in 1922 that the 6th Inniskilling Dragoons were merged with the 5th Dragoon Guards to form the 5th/6th Dragoons. This was very unpopular, I remember, and it was only resolved in 1935 when the King – George V – approved the renaming of the unit as the 5th Royal Inniskilling Dragoon Guards.

I married my wife, Ida, in 1930, and we had one daughter, Vera, who was born in 1933. We had a house built for us and we lived in it all our married life until Ida died.

During the Second World War I was a chartered accountant, which was a reserved occupation, and was director of a shipping yard in Hull. I had to sleep at the yard every night, as the bombing raids came in, and it was my responsibility, if the Germans landed and tried to take it, to blow it up.

When I retired I loved to go fishing, and often went over to Ireland to do this – but I never visited Inniskilling, which had been the home of my regiment. I used to travel a lot and I went on a cruise to America when I was almost ninety.

I was very honoured when, for my hundred-and-fifth birthday, the chairman and regimental secretary of the Royal Dragoon Guards Regimental Association, now based in York, came to my celebration. It was a wonderful occasion, with all my family – grandchildren and great-grandchildren – there.

Bert Clark

Northamptonshire Regiment · *Born* 20 November 1899, *died* 3 June 2006

I was born on 20 November 1899 at 70 Knox Road, Wellingborough. I had brothers: one younger and one eighteen months older than me and one who'd be about ten years older than me. I had three sisters too; we used to have big families then – seven was nothing. There was Sid, myself, Charlie and Fred – four of us boys.

I went to All Saints School, on the opposite side of the road from where the castle was in Wellingborough. I used to walk to school – it wasn't far to walk from Knox Road to the end of Castle Street. I don't think I did enjoy my schooling – because honestly speaking I was backward. In those days, if you got things wrong, they'd soon get the stick out to you – I either got the stick or the strap across the backside, with me lying across the desk.

There was not much sport going when we were eleven to thirteen, but what games we had we played on the Castle Field – a big park, there was a proper castle there, years and years ago. There was a big gang of us and we used to roll down the bank. Then there were big water pipes and we used to go across the brook on them. It was a mixed school – and we used to be together, boys and girls in the same class. We had slates and chalk, and books too – some of each. I left school in 1912, when I was thirteen.

I remember the *Titanic* going down. It was a great shock as we all thought it was such a marvellous ship.

In those days, on Saturday afternoons we'd go to the Palace Cinema – a penny to go in and it was all silent movies with someone playing the piano – oh yes, they were good. They'd be playing while us kids were creating hell. Then we'd buy a bag of sweets when we came out.

When I was thirteen I started work at Page's shoe factory in Wellingborough, but six months later we came to Rushden and I started work at Claridges, doing shoe work. At first I earned half a crown a week, working on a machine they called a moulder. You'd shape one shoe, get that one out and then you repeated it. I remember I smashed my fingers, but I carried on working – I was only fourteen.

In 1914 in Wellingborough, while I was working in the shoe factory, I saw a lot of my friends going off to war. I volunteered too, but they wouldn't have me because of my eyes. However, in 1917, I joined a volunteer force, and we were issued with uniforms and used to use a nearby garage as a drill room. When I was nineteen, I walked up to Bedford to Kempston Barracks, and joined up. I took my glasses off for the medical, and the doctor asked me if I wore them all the time – and then told me in no uncertain terms to put them back on. After that they asked what regiment I wanted to go into, and I said the Northants. So they sent me right back to Northampton for training in Barrack Road. The training was tough, but I was very fit then.

We went from there to Ireland, and we were there about twelve months. We used to go round in a lorry. We'd get one of these Sinn Fein blokes that we captured to stay in the front, and if there was any firing going on, he'd be the first to get it. You couldn't do that now, but in those days it was tit for tat – if they did something to us, we went back and did it to their people. I suppose it was the earliest days of terrorism. It was all confined to Ireland then. I went to Tipperary to the hospital – I had to go for an operation for a rupture – but that was another part of the country.

We did come under fire several times, actually. The first time we were walking along a country lane, and they came out of the ground – they'd dug in in different places. They'd fire at you as you were riding along. Two or three times a week we'd change platoons, and bike around the countryside. We were like sitting targets.

The platoon had had Lee Enfield Rifles – and we also had machine guns, mounted on a swivel. I was just an ordinary rifleman, but many's the time I had to open fire.

That was my first time away from home and I think I came back just once during that year. You had to bring all your kit, your rifle and everything with you. I'd been home about three days and got orders to return. We were meant to be home for fourteen days' leave, and we got just three.

If we went out with any Irish girls, the Irish people would have cut their hair off – we saw that happen a number of times. They'd do that just for speaking to a British soldier. We did sometimes visit local farms, and occasionally they'd give us home-made bread and butter, which tasted wonderful. We lived like that for eighteen months there, working together with the Irish police. One way and another I learnt some very saucy Irish songs while I was there.

I had no leave when I got back from Ireland. We went straight from Ireland to India. We were on the boat for three weeks. We left from Cork – I can remember going up the gangway to board. We were meant to sleep in hammocks on the boat, but I got on board and had five days and five nights lying out on top – just going to the edge of the boat and leaving my stomach behind. There is nothing worse. I remember that like it was yesterday. A pal of mine went to the place where they sold tea and got me a big mugful, and said, 'Get that down you,' and after that I was all right. It was just what I needed. Once we got to India it took us a week to get to our camps, stopping at different encampments on the way. I was still with the Northampton Regiment – the 48th/58th of Foot, at the time.

We were in India four years, before they decided to send about twenty of us home. I was there from when I was twenty to twenty-four. You couldn't go outside there during the day – it was too hot. First thing in the morning from about six to half past eight, you were on your drill, and then you were back indoors in the barracks.

We used to go out at night, down the bazaar. You see we owned India in those days, and where we were there was a big castle that we used to parade around. At one time we were at Amritsar, and we marched up the mountain to Dalhousie, and it certainly was damn lousy! We had to get a blowtorch to burn off the lice in our uniforms.

All this time I was still a private – I never got further than that. We didn't see any action in India – it was more policing – a matter of you just being there. There was a lot of fighting going on up the Khyber Pass, but we never went up there. It would have been very dangerous to venture up there.

We got on OK with the officers but they had to be pretty sharp. What would you expect? The troops were all Northants men, but I never found out where the officers came from. They might have come from the other end of England. We had men with us who fought in the First World War – it was allright with them – they were pleased enough to talk about it.

When we left India, we got to England and we were discharged with a civvy suit. We got home and it was hard to get a job then. That was 1924 and it was a bad year. I was on unemployment benefit for six weeks – then I went the next week and they said, 'Mr Clark, there's no money for you here. There's enough money going in the house to keep you.' I was only allowed to draw the dole for six weeks – and now they give it away!

It was getting on for twelve months before I got a job, and it was very depressing to come out of the forces and not find any work. I worked in a shoe factory all my life – the company John Whites. I worked for them for about thirty years, working on a machine called a pounder. When the uppers are put on the lathes the bottoms are all rough, so the pounder was a big emery wheel and you had to press the shoe on the wheel and smooth all the pleats out, so the sole was level for the outer sole to be stuck on. The machines tended to catch fire; when the tacks were still in, the dust would fly up into the extractor fan. Then, when a tack hit the emery wheel, the sparks used to set fire to the rising dust. It happened quite regularly.

I met my wife at the local fair – but I knew her when we were little, at school. She was in service, and at the fair she was with another girl who said, 'I know that chap.' Millie caught up with me – and after that we were courting for about five years – might even be a bit more. She finished up in service at a doctor's and I used to walk to Raunds and walk back with her. Many a time the bus had gone before we got to the stop, so I'd end up walking twenty-four

Bert Clark served in Northern Ireland and India, then left the Army in 1924. Pictured here at his wedding to Millie on 14 January 1928, they were married for nearly 66 years.

miles. We married in 1928 – she was a year and a week older than me. We had our little arguments – you can expect that – but we never had a row. We were married for sixty-five years, eleven months and two weeks. We moved into this home, and she had only been here about three weeks when she collapsed. They took her to Kettering, she was there for a week, and she never opened her eyes any more – but I don't think she suffered.

During the 1930s I worked for Walls Ice Cream, riding a 'Stop-me-and-buy-one' tricycle for about five years. One Christmas, in a snowstorm, I cycled about ten miles to Wickstead Park. I was stopped once on the way and sold half of a one-penny lolly. On the way back, the same child stopped me again for the other half, and that was all I sold that day.

In 1939 I was forty and I went on working in the factory. We were making mountain shoes with the spikes on the soles. Then during the war I became a volunteer fireman in the factory. I was in the shoe room and I'd just come back from going round the whole factory. A man came knocking at the door – this was Sunday morning – and he said, 'Did you know the factory's on fire?' Since I'd checked, the wind had turned round. There was a big slope and all the rubbish had swept up there during the day, and a spark had set it alight. It did a fair bit of damage on the upper level. Another time, a balloon came down and just missed my factory. It came down on a building opposite where they found a man on the roof – and his head somewhere else. Then it moved on and hit a hotel before our chaps could catch up with it and fetch it down. I was glad when that was all over, I can tell you. I went on working, then as soon as I turned sixty-five, I said, 'I'm finished.'

I used to smoke forty a day – when they had tubes of cigarettes.

I smoked until I was about thirty-five, when I gave up. There was a machine on the wall, five fags – Woodbines – for 2d. I did drink, but for the last twenty or thirty years I haven't been able to stand the smell of it. I used to drink and drink so I didn't know where I was. This was at the time when I worked for Walls. At the end of the season we used to go on an outing to a concert and one time I got so drunk, I was still drunk at the end of next week. I said, 'Never again!' And I can't stand the smell of it even now.

I don't know what I put my long life down to – I've just led a normal life. I never thought for one second I would see this age. I believe in the Father – my son thinks someone up there turned over two pages and missed me out – and I believe that eventually I'll see my Millie again.

Bill Stone

Royal Navy · *Born* 23 September 1900

I was born at Pound House in the hamlet of Ledstone, where they made cider, two miles north of Kingsbridge, South Devon, on 23 September 1900. This was before electricity or gas, so the house was lit with candles and oil lamps. I'm one of fourteen children, and I'm the tenth. I had eight sisters, and five brothers – fourteen of us, and I'm the last one left. They've all gone now. I tell everybody that I hope this new century is going to be as good as the last century. I tell you what – I haven't got an enemy in the world now. I've outlived them all! 'Keep going!', that's my motto.

My father used to ride a pony and trap round the farms. He used to do everything himself – he even killed pigs. Everyone kept a pig in those days. I went to Goveton School in the next little village about a mile away. Miss Collins was our head teacher, and the other teacher was Miss Gillard. There were just three in my class and only about twelve of us in the whole school. I started school when I was three and I was thirteen when I left.

We lived in the country, so we had fowls, chickens, and pigs – we ate well. We had eggs, chickens – lots of pork. My father used to keep two pigs. He said you mustn't have one pig – you must have two – they see who can eat the most and get fat quicker. Father would sell the two pigs and keep the heads, or half of the pig. We used to eat rabbits too.

I went to work on a farm when I was thirteen, for half a crown a week – with Farmer Giles on Sherford Down Farm, near a little place called Sherford. By 1915 – the first whole year of the war – I'd had two years on the farm. I lived on the farm with two others, about three miles away from home. The other two men were a couple of years older than me. When the war began, the oldest one joined the Royal Marines, and he got killed.

When I was fifteen, I walked to Kingsbridge to join the navy, because everyone was joining up. When my papers came, my father wouldn't sign them and he sent them back. He already had three sons in the war and he felt I was too young. Had he signed them, and I'd gone in then, I wouldn't be here today.

I did a variety of jobs, and when I was sixteen I was driving a water cart around the roads of Kingsbridge to damp down the dust, because it was before the days of tarmac. There was a pipe at the back with holes in which sprayed water over the surface, making a muddy cement, which we then rolled flat with a steam roller.

Just two weeks before I was eighteen, I was driving a big steam engine, hauling timber, and my father came to my work, and said, 'Your papers are at home to join the army.' But it wasn't to join the army – it was to go to Exeter to be medically examined. Then, when you were eighteen they'd call you up – it was conscription. So I got on my bike and caught the next train to Plymouth and joined the

navy. We were all naval men, you see. We had nothing to do with
the army. I sent the papers back to the army and they said, 'Where
did you join? What did you join?' I told them I was in the navy.
They called me up right on my birthday – 23 September. I only
served a couple of months in the first war, but I was doing it in
the navy.

At the end of the war on 11 November I was in hospital with flu
in barracks at Devonport. I had just started training then. Thousands
of sailors died of flu in Plymouth. They'd be on parade and they'd
just keel over. I fell on my head in my dinner. I didn't fall on the
deck, and maybe that saved me. I had a week to ten days in bed.
One day the doctor came around to the man next to me who said,
'I'm allright now.' He said, 'Fourteen days' leave,' So when he came
to me, I said, 'I'm allright, sir.' 'Fourteen days' leave.' It got you out
of the hospital. Our clothes all had to be fumigated. It was terrible. All
over the world, there was more died of flu than was killed in the
war.

I trained in the barracks for about three months. I'd joined as an
ordinary seaman, but my brothers were stokers and they asked me
what the hell I'd done that for. I said that I didn't know. So I transferred from an ordinary seaman to a stoker. My first ship was the
Tiger – a three-funnelled battlecruiser. I joined her at Rosyth in
Scotland.

We used to take in thousands of tons of coal at a time. It took a
day and a night to take it on and everyone joined in. The lighter
came alongside and the grab dumped it on the deck and we were
down in the bunkers, trimming. It was bloody awful. You've four
furnaces – two and two – and you cleaned out every one of them in
the course of twelve hours. You'd let them die down, crack up some

coal and clear out all the ash. Then you'd put in the coal that you'd broken up. The furnace next to the one you cleaned – you'd take out the burning coal with a shovel. We used to have flannel trousers to keep the heat off, and you had to wear a cap or a cap cover, because the steam pipes would be dripping, with condensation running down on your heads.

I'd take off my pants and vest after work and hang them on the rails, and when I went on watch the next time, my trousers would be standing up on their own, with the perspiration and coal dust. I used to take a little piece of coal and wash it and put it in my mouth to keep my mouth moist. I believe the miners used to do that as well. You'd be sucking that, and breathing through your nose, see? I was on the *Tiger* until 1922, and I was a stoker when I left. You're a stoker, and then you get made leading stoker – that's like a corporal. Then you get made petty officer, and that's like a sergeant. If you're the chief petty officer, you're like a sergeant major.

I went to the *Hood* in 1922 and did an eleven-month cruise round the world as part of the Special Service Squadron on the Empire Cruise – that was wonderful. There was the *Hood* and the *Repulse*, and we went to the Canary Islands, down the west coast of Africa. The seamen who had not crossed the Equator before went through the 'crossing the line' ceremony. We were sailing to 'show the flag' to the colonies, and on board we carried a Rolls-Royce, complete with driver for the official visits ashore. We went on to Ceylon, Singapore, Indonesia and then to Fremantle, Adelaide and Melbourne in Australia, and Hobart in Tasmania. The captain had orders to give all the ship's company as much leave as possible in any harbour where they had relatives. When we went to Wellington, New Zealand, I had an uncle there, so I got fourteen days' leave. It was smashing.

The fleet sailed on to Canada and the west coast of America, and the *Hood* continued alone through the Panama Canal. Sometimes there were only inches to spare between the ship and the sides of the canal itself.

After the *Hood*, I was about twenty-four – these were some of the best years of my life. I went to different ships – and on every ship I was on, I was the ship's barber. That started when I went to the *Hood*. The old chief who had retired said, 'Here boy, do you want to buy some clippers? Numbers one, two and three? And comb and scissors? A pound.' I said OK, and bought them, and started working on the flats down below. They all used to come to me – it was lovely. However, we had a proper barber's shop there. The man who was running it, as a seaman he was excused, and he was there all day – but he couldn't cut butter, and they didn't like the way he cut hair, and they shoved him out. They said, 'You take it on' – so I did. This was just in my spare time, you know – I had to do my own job too, but I didn't mind. It was sixpence a time mostly, and the chiefs and petty officers, rather than give me sixpence, would give me their tobacco. I had some interesting customers – Admiral Evans, 'Evans of the Broke', and Major Franco, the brother of General Franco. That was after I joined the *Eagle* – an aircraft carrier – in 1929, and we rescued him and his aircrew after their plane had had to ditch after running out of fuel.

When the *Hood* went down in 1941 it was terrible. I was on leave that day, and I didn't believe it – it was terrible. I still go to the *Hood* Association gatherings, and there's a dear old lady who's two months younger than me. She lost her son who was eighteen on the *Hood*. She said, 'I cried, and I cried and I cried.' I said, 'I'll tell you something that will buck you up. They've made a brass plaque,

Stoker First Class Bill Stone (seated) remained in the navy after the war and served on HMS *Hood* from 1922, then in 1925 was aboard HMS *Chrysanthemum*, with which ship he visited Malta, where this portrait was taken.

and they've got the names of all the men who went down in her on this plaque. They've lowered it down to the sunken ship, as near to the fo'c's'le – the bows – as possible and it will act as a headstone to a graveyard.' She said that that was lovely – a marvellous remembrance.

In 1931 I went to the *Harebell*, which was a sloop in fishery protection. The skipper was a crafty bastard; he'd go in harbour and he'd give half the ship's crew leave, and as soon as they'd gone, he'd get up steam and go and catch some fish. I'd say that it was nothing to do with me – it was down to the skipper.

From 1937 I was on the *Salamander*, which was a minesweeper. It was while I was with her that I got married to Lily – who was a local girl from near my home. Our daughter Anne was born at Portland a week before the war started in 1939. In 1940 we went to Dunkirk five times, bringing soldiers back from there to Dover – around two or three hundred at a time. We got hit several times. It was hell. I was regulating chief – the chief stoker in charge of all the stokers – and I was on the quarterdeck, hauling the soldiers in. One poor old soldier, his bones were sticking out of his legs and I managed to get a rope round him, but the ship went on and pulled him away – and we lost him. It was terrible. I remember saying, 'God help us' – and He did. I tell everybody that – if you're in difficulty, just say, 'God help us' and it goes a long way. It's a great consolation – it was my little prayer. We took on nearly three hundred at a time – so we brought back fifteen hundred or so altogether. We helped them aboard – some had no clothes at all and had swum out naked. One sailor said, 'Chief, one of them's gone up the gangway with your coat!' and I said, 'Good luck to him.' They were tired out and as they were coming down to the water's edge they were being bombed. In their panic they were digging themselves into the sand. It was terrible.

We went up and down the harbour, because we were a mine-sweeper, and we picked them up from the mole inside the harbour. We were all night picking them up, then taking them to Dover.

After Dunkirk, I stayed with the *Salamander*, and went up to Archangel. We were minesweeping there, off the coast of Russia. Then on the way back to Plymouth they said, 'Chief, you're going to leave the ship.' 'I don't want to leave the ship,' I said, I requested to see the commander. He said, 'Chief, you've been in the ship six years – you're due to leave.' He did me a favour, because the *Salamander* nearly got smashed to pieces. While she was off the coast of France, they should have received the signal to shift positions the next day – but they never got it, and she was attacked by our own bombers. Two or three minesweepers were sunk, and the *Salamander* was badly damaged.

I then went into the barracks, and I'd only been there a week, and the chief said, 'Good morning, Bill,' and I said, 'Good morning be buggered.' He said, 'What's wrong with you, you silly old sod?' I said, 'I've got a draft here,' and he said, 'So have I. We're going to Wallsend – a ship called the *Newfoundland* is being built.' He said that when a ship's being built, they send so many crew for twelve months, to see what's going on and to help them – to make suggestions and so on, and to report back to the commander. So for nearly twelve months I was in harbour, and that was nice.

After that we were convoying, then we went to Bone, in North Africa. When the Allies made the landing at Sicily, we were there, bombarding the bay for three days. Then we went back to Malta, taking on provisions – and while we were there we had a visit from

General Montgomery. The last trip back we were torpedoed by an Italian submarine. It cut our stern off, and with it the rudder, so we couldn't steer. They patched us up temporarily in Malta, and we steamed to America with no rudder – we steered with the engines. Of course it was difficult, because we joined a convoy which only did about seven knots, but eventually we got to America, and that was good. It was after that that I got a Mention in Dispatches.

Sicily was my last action, and eventually I returned with the ship from America, but then I left her because I was forty-four. I was about the oldest man on the ship. The officer kept saying, 'Are you going to volunteer to come with us, Chief?' And I said, 'No, I don't volunteer for anything, I'm like a wheelbarrow – I go where I'm pushed.'

A week before the armistice was signed, I had a week's training with a revolver, then we were sent to North Germany to guard the island of Sylt in case there was trouble. We went to Ostend then soldiers took us right up to the north of Germany. After that we came back to Plymouth, and I was demobbed after twenty-seven years in the navy.

When I left the navy I became a hairdresser. I was supposed to go to one of those big stores, because they used to have barbers in the store. But when I got demobbed, I took my family to Yorkshire for a holiday, but when I came back it was too late and someone else had taken it. So I worked in a barber's shop for about a month, and one day, as I was walking along the street, my wife said, 'Look here, "Hair dresser and tobacconist for sale. Paignton".' My wife's cousin owned a business in Plymouth, so one afternoon we went up and inspected the shop. It only had two chairs. It cost about £2000 and I paid a £10 deposit. A week later, everything was sorted. I worked there from 1945 for twenty-three years. We used to live over the shop until we got more prosperous and then we bought a lovely house overlooking Torbay. We only had the one daughter. Lily, my wife, had an awful labour. I like children and I'd like to have had more, but now I have two grandchildren, Susie and Christopher. Lily's health declined in 1986, and we moved to Watlington in Oxford-shire to be near the family, until she died in 1995.

My mother never worried about anything. In 1951, when she was eighty-seven, my father died and I used to go and see her occa-sionally. She said, 'Do you miss Father?' and I said I did. She said, 'I don't.' I said, 'Why not?' and she said, 'Well, I always said I wished Father would go first, because if I go first, there will be no one to look after him.' She said, 'I've had my wish.' She never bothered about us getting on – she knew we'd be all right.

My weight was always 11 stone 7 – except for one short period in 1929 when I went up to 14 stone. My favourite meal now is dinner at midday. I used to smoke like hell, and drink like mad. I haven't smoked now for about sixty years. 'Filthy habit,' we used to say. But during the war I smoked – Woodbines – about twenty or thirty a day. I'll tell you a little story. When I was a boy, Mother used to give my brother and me a penny each to put in the church collection box. One day we went into the post office in Goveton which sold cigarettes. We bought a packet of Woodbines for a penny. You got five Woodbines for a penny. So then we said, 'Our sister will tell Mother we haven't put the money in the collection box. What are we going to do?' I said, 'I know. We'll go back to the shop again and ask them for two halfpennies for the penny.' So we both put a halfpenny into the collection box. I smoked a clay pipe for a while, but one day, when the ship was rolling, I dropped it over the ruddy side. For years after that I wouldn't smoke in the ship – there was always trouble if I did. But as soon as I went ashore and had a drink, I had to have a cigarette.

I'll tell you another story. In Buenos Aires we had hundreds of people come aboard, and my friend and I saw these two nice girls and thought we'd show them around. They said, 'We'd like to meet you when you come ashore.' So when we got ashore, they were waiting with a car and took us for a drive. It was one of those cars where you sit in the back – all open. All of a sudden it stopped dead. I said, 'What have you stopped for?' One of them said, 'You know the meaning of Buenos Aires?' 'No, not really.' 'Well, Buenos is good, and Aires is air – good air, and you sailors are smoking those beastly cigarettes.' So we threw them over the side. The story carries on – we went to their house – they were lovely people. And they drove us back to the ship about eight o'clock at night. They said, 'You will write to us, won't you?' We said, 'Yes – but we haven't got your address.' I said, 'I know, I've got my Players packet' – and I wrote their address on this Players packet and went aboard. The next day, of course I smoked the cigarettes one after another, and threw the blooming packet over the side. I was sorry, because they were real good girls. People would say, did you have a girl in every port, and I'd say no – two.

I think of the *Hood*, she should never have taken part in that war – there was insufficient armour on her deck. They were going to put more armour on her, but they said that if they did, it would reduce her speed. When the *Bismarck* fired and caused a lot of fires, the open magazines to the 6-inch guns caught fire and all the magazines just blew up simultaneously. She broke in half in just under three minutes. One thousand four hundred men on board and only three survived. One of them was a man called Ted Briggs, and I met him at a *Hood* reunion and shook his hand. He said, 'Bill, how the hell do you keep so bloody young?' Ted told me that when the ship sank, he was underwater. He said to himself, 'I'm not going to drown,' and there was an explosion aboard when the ship sank and it blew him to the surface. I just told him that someone must be looking after both of us.

At that *Hood* Association gathering I sang this song:

All the nice girls love a sailor – all the nice girls love a tar,
Cos there's something about a sailor, for you know what the sailors are.
Fair and breezy, nice and easy – he's a lady's pride and joy.
He falls in love with Kate and Jane then he's off to sea again,
Ship ahoy, ship ahoy.

I sang it again in church on the following Sunday. The vicar said, 'Come on, William, sing that song that you sang at the club.' 'What, in church?' He said "Yes" – so I sang it. And they all clapped. Then I said, 'To please you all, I'll sing a verse from my favourite hymn, "Abide with Me",' and at the end, it says, 'in life, in death, oh Lord abide with me'. Later on, Ted Briggs said to my daughter, 'When your daddy sang that, I had a lump in my throat.'

I had three brothers who all did their full time in the navy, and four uncles who did their full time back in the eighteen hundreds. Eight of us who did our full time in the Royal Navy – all came out without a scratch. How lucky can you be?

These days I keep busy as a member of the Royal British Legion, the Dunkirk Veterans', Royal Naval, HMS *Hood*, HMS *Newfoundland* and Malta George Cross Island Associations and I enjoy my guest visits to the Western Front Association. In the last few years I met the Queen Mother, who said, 'You're a wonderful man.' We compared our birthdates and she told me she was about a month older than me. I also meet the Queen and Prince Philip, and Prince Charles and Princess Anne.

I've had an extraordinary life – a lucky life. Someone's looked after me, I'm sure. I believe in God and I say my little prayer every night. My wife taught me what to say: 'Lord keep us safe this night, secure from all our fears, may angels guard us while we sleep till morning light appears.' I used to say that in the navy, and I still say it. Even when I was chief petty officer, I still said it, yes – just to myself. There was the ship being hit, and I was firing at the Germans with a rifle, they were coming down so bloody low – and I survived it all.

Index